Advances in Consumer Marketing

Titles in the Cranfield Management Research Series include:

The Challenge of Strategic Management
Corporate Strategy and Financial Decisions
Strategic Marketing Planning
Strategy Planning in Logistics and Transportation
Making Sense of Competition Policy
European Developments in Human Resource Management
Executive Redundancy and Outplacement
The Challenge of International Business
The Future of Services Management
Advances in Consumer Marketing

These books are available from all good bookshops or directly from Kogan Page Ltd, 120 Pentonville Road, London N1 9JN.
Tel: 071 278 0433 Fax 071 837 6348

Advances
in Consumer
Marketing

Edited by
Mark Jenkins and
Simon Knox

First published in 1994

Kogan Page Limited
120 Pentonville Road
London N1 9JN

© Mark Jenkins and Simon Knox, 1994

British Library Cataloguing in Publication Data

A CIP record for this book is available from the British Library.

ISBN 0 7494 1127 9

Typeset by Books Unlimited (Nottm), Sutton-in-Ashfield, NG17 1AL
Printed in England by Clays Ltd, St Ives plc

CONTENTS

Contents

PART TWO – Managing Consumer Markets

PART THREE – Strategic Issues in Consumer Marketing

LIST OF FIGURES

LIST OF TABLES

THE CRANFIELD MANAGEMENT RESEARCH SERIES

The Cranfield Management Research Series represents an exciting joint initiative between the Cranfield School of Management and Kogan Page.

As one of Europe's leading post-graduate business schools, Cranfield is renowned for its applied research activities, which cover a wide range of issues relating to the practice of management.

Each title in the Series is based on current research and written by members of the Cranfield faculty or their associates. Many of the research projects have been undertaken with the sponsorship and active assistance of organisations from the industrial, commercial or public sectors. The aim of the series is to make the findings of direct relevance to managers through texts which are academically sound, accessible and practical.

For managers and academics alike, the Cranfield Management Research Series will provide access to up-to-date management thinking from some of Europe's leading academics and practitioners. The series represents both Cranfield's and Kogan Page's commitment to furthering the improvement of management practice in all types of organisations.

THE SERIES EDITORS

Frank Fishwick
Reader in Managerial Economics
Director of Admissions at Cranfield School of Management

Dr Fishwick joined Cranfield from Aston University in 1966, having previously worked in textiles, electronics and local government (town and country planning). Recent research and consultancy interests have been focused on business concentration, competition policy and the book publishing industry. He has been directing a series of research studies for the Commission of the European Communities, working in collaboration with business economists in France and Germany. He is permanent economic adviser to the Publishers Association in the UK and is a regular consultant to other public and private sector organisations in the UK, continental Europe and the US.

Gerry Johnson
Professor of Strategic Management
Director of the Centre for Strategic Management and Organisational Change
Director of Research at Cranfield School of Management

After graduating from University College London, Professor Johnson worked for several years in management positions in Unilever and Reed International and then became a management consultant. Since 1976, he has taught at Aston University Management Centre, Manchester Business School, and from 1988 at Cranfield School of Management. His research work is primarily concerned with processes of strategic decision making and strategic change in organisations. He also works as a consultant on issues of strategy formulation change at a senior level with a number of UK and international firms.

Shaun Tyson
Professor of Human Resource Management
Director of the Human Resource Research Centre
Dean of the Faculty of Management and Administration at Cranfield School of Management

Professor Tyson studied at London University and spent eleven years in senior positions in industry within engineering and electronic companies.

For four years he was a lecturer in personnel management at the Civil Service College, and joined Cranfield in 1979. He has acted as a consultant and researched widely into human resource strategies, policies and the evaluation of the function. He has published fourteen books.

1

INTRODUCTION: CONTEMPORARY RESEARCH THEMES

Mark Jenkins and Simon Knox

Ever since the concept of marketing was accepted as a core business practice, consumer marketing has been at the cutting edge in theory development and practical application. The reasons for this are simple: the customer base is diffuse, heterogeneous and variety seeking, the competitive pressures are intense; and the channels for distributing manufacturers' brands to market are highly concentrated. Many marketing practitioners believe that consumers choose their brands in a highly discriminating and deliberate fashion, none more so than the manufacturers of grocery products. Consequently, manufacturer investment in building their brand's added-values can be a significant component of the cost of goods sold. Recently, a management consultant group estimated that this cost could be as much as 25 per cent, for a major food manufacturer. However, manufacturers' strategy of building strong grocery brands is being increasingly challenged by the development of own-label brands with the grocery retailer's marque. In the UK, the market with the highest level of own-label penetration, the market share is currently 33 per cent and is likely to rise to 40 per cent towards the year 2000.

A BROADER UNDERSTANDING OF CONSUMER MARKETING

Whilst many marketing texts consider the manufacturer-brand-consumer relationship, through an interpretation of strategic marketing management activities and the resultant consumer behaviour, few address the role of retailing, the brands and their relationships with both consumers and manufacturers. Still fewer texts attempt to do this from an empirical research base. In developing this book in consumer marketing, we have attempted to bring these elements together in a understandable and considered fashion. As a result, we believe the model which has emerged as an explanatory framework for this text provides a comprehensive and appropriate paradigm for understanding and managing consumer markets in the 1990s.

We believe that management literature requires a greater level of integration and interpretation from this interactive perspective, than it has had up to now. Whilst the consumer must still remain a focal element, attitudinal and behavioural understanding of purchase decisions are not sufficient, in isolation, to enable the consumer-based marketing manager to do his or her job effectively. The role of the brand- and own-labels, their interpretation by consumers, manufacturers and retailers all need to be more effectively connected. For example, intermediaries can no longer simply provide a conduit between manufacturer and consumer. In the grocery sector, retailers are now regarded as the most powerful element within the value chain. They are, therefore, customers, rather than simply distribution points, and have become firmly established as buying agents for the consumer, rather than selling agents for the manufacturers.

The different chapters of this book explore these and other idiosyncrasies of consumer marketing – a management process distinctive from other markets and styles of marketing management. Hopefully, by accentuating these differences in the consumer marketing domain, we can assist in opening the door to more imaginative and creative management approaches.

Our interpretation has led us to propose a four-element model of the consumer marketing process (Figure 1.1). Whilst we acknowledge that the four elements of consumer, retailer, brand and manufacturer are important in themselves, it is their linkages and interactions which effectively define the management process.

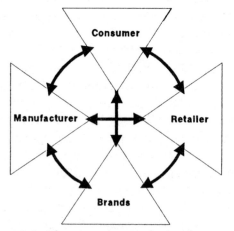

Figure 1.1 The consumer marketing framework

THE WHOLE IS GREATER THAN THE SUM OF THE PARTS...

The research presented in this book is not intended to be a comprehensive review, more a selection of key issues which allow a wider interpretation and encourage a broadening of the paradigm of consumer marketing. Individually, they will focus on different components of the model but together they do provide a new context for the challenge of managing these markets. All the research has been undertaken by academics and practitioners associated with the Cranfield School of Management who are currently engaged in the theoretical and practical development of consumer marketing. As a necessary condition for inclusion each contribution has been successfully submitted to peer group review. Whilst this fact alone does not automatically guarantee relevance or immediate applicability to practising managers, it does mean that the research has been undertaken on a rigorous basis and builds on an established position within the current body of research. Much of the research is new. A small number of contributions have already been published elsewhere. These have been included because we believe that the issues they raise are just as relevant today as when they were then.

STRUCTURE AND CONTENT

Each chapter is prefaced by an outline of the key points and the context of the research. The chapters are grouped within three parts. Part one, 'Understanding Consumer Perspectives of Brands and the Purchasing Environment', focuses on the consumer marketing framework from the perspective of the consumer, and their interpretation of loyalty, retail location, merchandising and pricing. Chapters 2 and 3 focus on the linkage between consumers and retailer. Initially, Tim Denison and Simon Knox highlight the importance of consumer loyalty to retail businesses and discuss the problems inherent in defining and measuring this concept. Their 'double indemnity' effect, particular to grocery retailing, underlines the potential benefits of marketing strategies which centre on the loyal shopper through customer retention. Following on from this chapter, Gordon Foxall and Paul Hackett explore how consumers 'wayfind' particular stores, discussing the implication of retail location in both planned and unplanned sites and the role of primary attractors in drawing consumers to adjacent stores.

The concluding chapters of Part one are concerned with the linkage between the consumer and the brand. In Chapter 4, Simon Knox explores grocery shopping protocols through to point of purchase in the retail environment and the differences in purchasing styles between frequent and occasional shoppers for particular brands and own-labels. Following on from this chapter Simon Knox and Leslie de Chernatony focus on the changing value assessment of a brand, as perceived by the consumer, when a product category develops from a niche to a mass market. The final contribution to this section attempts to broaden the interpretation of the model through a paper which links each component: consumer, brand, retailer and manufacturer. Leslie de Chernatony, Simon Knox and Mark Chedgey present a comparative study of consumer perceptions of brand-leader and own-label pricing policies in contrasting markets.

Part two, 'Managing Consumer Markets', discusses how marketing managers can enhance their role through effective marketing research, in order to: understand the consumer, strengthen the brand; and manage crises. Initially, Stephen King discusses how managers should broaden the concept of the brand and why they need to find structural and non-structural approaches to link understanding of the consumer across the organisation. A highly practical example of crisis management in the context of brand withdrawal is provided by Craig Smith and his co-authors in Chapter 8. The problems associated with this process are delineated and the wider lessons for managers are drawn. The final contribution is once more provided by Stephen King who in Chapter 9 tackles the management issue of how our understanding of the consumer can be translated to decision making. Whilst these thoughts were penned a number of years ago, this paper raises issues which are still highly relevant to the consumer markets of the 1990s.

Part three, 'Strategic Issues in Consumer Marketing', pulls together a number of contemporary themes. In Chapter 10, Keith Thompson provides a perspective and suggested explanations for the strategies of UK retailers in the context of the Single European Grocery Market; the dynamics within this sector will have far-reaching consequences for both transnational and regional competition. The contributors to Chapters 11 and 12 adopt an organisational perspective and focus on what is to be gained by managers reinterpreting markets and adopting a more systematic approach to creative thinking. Mark Jenkins and co-authors surface and discuss concerns relating to the fact that, for many fast-moving consumer goods (fmcg) organisations, the consumer is less than central to their definition of the market. The final contribution is written by Simon Majaro who provides a macro-perspective on the potential of organisational creativity and innovation, both of which are central tenets to successful consumer marketing. He discusses how such energy can be utilised and channelled within the organisation.

Whilst all these themes relate to different interactions of the consumer marketing framework, in structuring the book this way, the reader is able to move from a consumer to a managerial perspective. We do not claim that the managerial issues raised here are dealt with exhaustively, but we do think they illustrate graphically the integrated nature of consumer markets and the dynamics of the structural elements. As the Single European Consumer Market develops in competitive intensity, and structural complexity increases, it is only those managers who fully appreciate the nature of these market characteristics and change agents that will develop their brand portfolios successfully.

The book is aimed at two categories of reader. The first is practising managers who wish to update themselves, without having to scan volumes of academic journals. We believe that all the chapters are accessible and succinct, providing insights into important management issues at both the operational and strategic levels.

The second reader type is likely to be the student or academic who wishes to explore the changing nature of consumer marketing from the empirical research and theory development point of view. We believe that our framework will broaden, and help them to re-evaluate, their understanding of consumer marketing.

Our thanks go to the people who have permitted us to include their work in this book. In addition to the Cranfield School of Management, a number of other premier universities are represented including Georgetown University and the Harvard Business School in the United States. We hope this book will be as interesting and enjoyable to read as it was to create.

PART ONE

UNDERSTANDING CONSUMER PERSPECTIVES OF BRANDS AND THE PURCHASING ENVIRONMENT

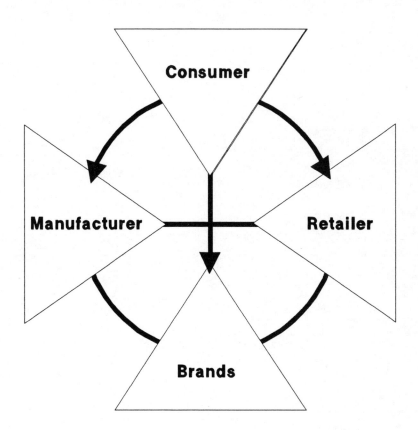

2

POCKETING THE CHANGE FROM LOYAL SHOPPERS: THE 'DOUBLE INDEMNITY' EFFECT[*]

Tim Denison and Simon Knox

OUTLINE

Over the last two decades, we have witnessed a movement in channel power away from manufacturers towards retailers. Today, consumer buying behaviour and shopping protocols are influenced far less by the pull of proprietary brands. In contrast, the profile and stature of major retailers amongst consumers has continued to grow.

Despite this change, the subject of store loyalty is one that has attracted less attention among academics than brand loyalty. In contrast, commercial retailers have not overlooked the strategic importance of customer loyalty. Faced with market maturity and recession, there is considerable current interest among retailers in loyalty schemes as a means of shoring up customer bases and securing market share.

Our contribution to this book is built around an empirical study of the shopping habits of 750 consumers. The chapter addresses a series of basic questions:

- What do we mean by store loyalty and how do we measure it?
- Do loyalty levels vary across retail sectors?
- Does it pay for retailers to have a loyal customer base?

All our results underline the fact that loyal customers are potentially more profitable to retailers and highlight the increasing strategic and operational importance of loyalty programmes across all retail sectors during the 1990s as market saturation is reached.

---

* An earlier version of this chapter was presented at the Marketing Education Group 1993 Conference, 'Emerging Issues in Marketing', Loughborough University Business School.

INTRODUCTION

Manufacturers of fast-moving consumer goods (fmcgs) have long been aware of the importance of customer loyalty to their brands. This has been the focus of numerous academic and business models since the 1950s in which links between brand loyalty and indicators of market performance, such as market share, have been established (Ehrenberg et al 1990). In contrast, retailers have traditionally placed less strategic importance on customer loyalty (Wrigley and Dunn 1984c).

However, even the most powerful of business enterprises cannot ignore the natural forces of change. With the recent decline in retail sales as market saturation is reached, coupled with the need actually to raise sales volume to spread higher fixed cost investments (such as larger sites and electronic data systems), competition amongst major retailers has intensified (Knee and Walters 1985; Richards and Smiddy 1985). Though store location remains the keystone to gaining customers, there is growing belief in the value of keeping them loyal. Retail management efforts to do just this are becoming increasingly commonplace, through loyalty clubs, cards and programmes, each designed to motivate the consumer to spend more in one store group and less in others. However, absolute customer loyalty, at store level, is not a realistic proposition for retail marketers. Whilst consumers may conceivably retain the services of the same high street bank throughout their working life, possibly at the exclusion of all others, it is inconceivable that they would show comparable loyalty to a grocery multiple or clothing chain. Research suggests that most shoppers are notoriously 'promiscuous', switching from store to store at will (Kau and Ehrenberg 1984). For the retailer, the challenge rests in raising the degree of customer loyalty rather than winning over lifetime exclusivity.

Marketing investment in long-term customer relationships is finding favour across many industries, particularly within the service sector where, traditionally, marketing effort has been concentrated on attracting new customers rather than keeping existing ones. The wisdom of customer retention strategies in, for example, the banking and insurance sectors is beyond doubt; the high initial costs of setting up new accounts are offset through subsequent transactions over the lifetime of the relationship. According to Christopher et al (1991) retaining customer accounts in these circumstances is the key to profitability. Any increase in lifetime of the customer relationship with the firm can lead to substantial improvements in business performance. For example, Reichhold and Sasser (1990) found that, by reducing customer defections by 10 per cent, a credit card company increased its profitability by over 120 per cent. They also found that a 5 per cent cut in defections resulted in an 85 per cent increase in profits for a bank's branch system and a 50 per cent increase in an insurance brokerage. However, the relationship between customer loyalty and business profitability in the retailing of fmcgs or durables has not been widely studied.

In this chapter, we present some significant findings about store loyalty and consumer spend amongst these types of retail outlets, based upon an empirical study of UK shopping behaviour. We address two main issues. Firstly, we explore the extent to which consumers are loyal to particular stores at a time when consumer mobility and store choice have never been so great. Secondly, we examine the relationship between the levels of store loyalty and consumer spend across five retail sectors, to establish conclusively whether or not they are linked in the retailing of goods as they appear to be in the retailing of services.

MEASURING STORE LOYALTY

Many past studies of consumer loyalty and buyer behaviour have concentrated on the dual issues of repeat purchase and brand choice (eg see Chatfield et al 1966; Ehrenberg 1988; Goodhardt et al 1984). They reflected the overriding power that manufacturers enjoyed over retailers in facilitating consumer choice during the 1960s and early 1970s. Consumer buying behaviour was heavily influenced by the pull of manufacturers' proprietary brands rather than by the push of retailers.

Nowadays, this situation has reversed; channel power clearly lies with retailers (Knox and White 1991). It appears that consumer buying behaviour is influenced at least as much by the retailer as the manufacturer, as the growing market share of own-label brands suggests (de Chernatony and MacDonald 1992). For this reason the topic of store loyalty and shopping protocol has begun to attract research attention (see Kau and Ehrenberg 1984; Knox and de Chernatony 1990), though brand choice at point of sale continues to be a dominant theme.

So what is meant by store loyalty? In essence, it refers to the consumer's inclination to patronise a given store or chain of stores over time. Whilst expressions of store loyalty and customer retention are often used as a surrogate for buying behaviour patterns, they are often used imprecisely. Since consumers are very rarely exclusively loyal to a store group, in practice store loyalty is a relative term and so is more difficult to measure precisely. Many analysts choose to use the measure of repeat store visits as a convenient expression for store loyalty, despite the obvious

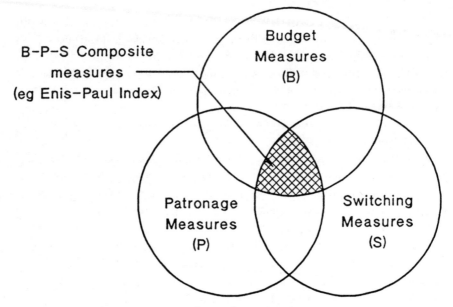

Figure 2.1 A typology of store loyalty measures

shortcoming of the disregard for store spend. Who is the more loyal shopper? Is it the person who visits the same store on seven out of every ten grocery shopping trips or the person who only goes there every fourth trip but buys 80 per cent of their food there?

Various measures of store loyalty have been used in past studies. Some were originally developed for assessing brand loyalty, others are more original and tailored to store behaviour. In a sense, the fact that multiple measures exist at all reflects the lack of a coherent definition. We have classified them into four categories (see Figure 2.1).

Measure 1: the patronage ratio (P)

Store loyalty can be measured simply by comparing the number of purchases made in one store for a particular product line relative to other stores. Both Kelley (1967) and Thompson (1967) have adopted this approach. It is also the basis upon which store choice is considered in the stochastic models of buyer behaviour which have come to dominate brand choice and repeat buying studies (Jephcott 1972; Wrigley 1980; Kau 1981; Kau and Ehrenberg 1984; Wrigley and Dunn 1984b, 1984c; Ehrenberg 1988; Lamb and Goodhardt 1989).

However, simply measuring store patronage over time fails to capture any change of allegiance that may have taken place during that time. For example, consumer A may regularly shop interchangeably between stores 1 and 2, say, over a six-month period, showing little loyalty preference between the two. Compare this to a situation in which consumer B shops continually at store 1 for three months and then becomes disillusioned with it, so abandoning it for store 2 during the remainder of the study period. With regard to patronage over the full six-month period, both exhibit an equal level of loyalty, but their behavioural patterns are very different, and this must be accounted for in a true measure of loyalty.

This illustration demonstrates the problem of any measure of store loyalty which is based upon frequency of visit (or store patronage) alone. Clearly this weakness is more pronounced over longer study periods as consumers' long-term commitment to a particular store diminishes and gives way to other preferences.

Measure 2: the switching ratio (S)

Farley (1968) and Rao (1969) were amongst the earliest to criticise the patronage measure in the context of store loyalty and offer an alternative which reflected the degree of 'switching' between favoured stores over time. This involves measuring the number of successive visits or 'runs' to the same store/store chain. Crouchley et al (1982a, 1982b) have adopted this means to measure store loyalty more recently.

Measure 3: the budget ratio (B)

The main advocate of this approach has been Cunningham (1956, 1961) who measured loyalty in terms of the proportion of the consumer's total expenditure on groceries made in the consumer's 'first choice' store. More recently Dunn and Wrigley (1984) have followed Cunningham's approach. The advantage of this measure is that it takes into account the relative level of spend, whereas any 'analysis by purchase occasion' (using either patronage or switching measures) does not differentiate between 'main' shopping trips and 'top-up' trips.

To many analysts, expenditure patterns are the most appealing single measure of store loyalty, but the measure is not without its weaknesses. For example, were a consumer to shop regularly for everyday clothes in store A but, occasionally, buy expensive designer wear elsewhere, an analysis by expenditure alone would not clearly establish underlying loyalty to store A.

Measure 4: composite measures (B-P-S)

Tate (1961), recognising the shortcomings of the single measure, used a composite index: the number of stores visited and the proportion spent at the 'first choice' store. Others, notably Carmen (1970) and Enis and Paul (1970), have also followed this example by developing index measures.

The Enis-Paul Index

The Enis-Paul measure consists of an unweighted, geometric mean of patronage, switching and budget measures applied to the 'first choice' store. It is calculated as a percentage figure which ranges from the theoretical upper limit of 100 per cent, indicating exclusive purchasing at one store throughout the study period, towards the zero lower limit, indicating complete 'promiscuity'. In practice, values will rarely fall below 5 per cent since the measure is applied to the store in which the consumer spends most over the study period (ie 'first choice' store). The precise formula of the Enis-Paul Index is detailed at the end of the chapter.

Though such a measure is multi-dimensional and offers a more balanced model of loyal behaviour, it also suffers from being less straightforward to interpret than the single measures. Consumers who are deemed 60 per cent loyal to their 'first choice' store, using an expenditure measure, are said to spend 60 per cent of their budget in that store. However, using a composite measure no such direct conclusions can be drawn. A high loyalty rating is generally indicative of a high budget percentage, patronage of few stores and infrequent switching. A very high value for one of these measures can offset a low value of another, as Figure 2.2 illustrates.

Charton (1973), in his excellent review of empirical developments in store loyalty, argues that the value of any single or composite measure rests on its usefulness in application. Given that our research objective was to provide a comparative measure of store loyalty levels across five

100 ◄────────── Enis–Paul Index Value ──────────► 0

◄──── Higher ───── % Spend in first choice store ───── Lower ────►

◄──── Lower ───── Number of stores patronised ───── Higher ────►

◄──── Lower ── Amount of "switching" between stores ── Higher ────►

◄────────── "Loyal" ────────────── "Promiscuous" ────────►

Figure 2.2 Characteristics of the Enis-Paul measure

retail sectors with very different patterns of consumer expenditure, choice and frequency of visit, the Enis-Paul Index seemed to us the most enabling in these circumstances. Our full research rationale and design is discussed in the next section.

RESEARCH METHODOLOGY

Leaving aside this problem of loyalty definition and measure, there seemed to us a number of compelling reasons why we should carry out this new empirical study at this time.

Firstly, it is now ten years since the last UK study of its kind was conducted by Wrigley and Dunn. Retailing has evolved considerably during the decade. On the one hand, consumers contrive to become more mobile and better informed which discourages strong loyalty to individual stores. On the other hand, major retailers have invested heavily in site location and image building, to differentiate themselves from competing stores and to target consumer groups more effectively (de Chernatony, Knox and Chedgey 1992). The physical shopping environment also continues to change: away from town centre locations towards planned and specialised shopping centres designed to encourage more pedestrian flow between the stores. It is unclear what overall impact these developments have had on store loyalty levels.

In our research design, we decided to measure store loyalty at ten major shopping centres exclusively, rather than in the high street, to reflect contemporary shopping behaviour, based around the car-owner rather than the pedestrian shopper.

Secondly, in most previous studies the researchers have focussed on grocery retailing in the USA or UK. It struck us that there was a real need to broaden the scope of existing knowledge by examining store loyalty across a range of retail sectors, if only to confirm that the conclusions reached from grocery-based studies do apply equally to other forms of retailing. So we designed our research to cover stores across the retail sectors, namely:

- petrol
- groceries
- DIY
- mixed retail
- department stores.

In the case of department and mixed retail stores, our pilot study showed measuring store loyalty is altogether a more diffuse task than in other sectors where product lines are more focussed (such as grocery or DIY goods). For some product lines, such as cosmetics, a respondent might be relatively loyal to a department store, but for many other lines sold there, they may be no more than an occasional buyer. So it is perhaps less appropriate to consider store loyalty per se in these types of store than to consider store loyalty with regard to particular product lines. This is the approach we adopted in assigning loyalty levels to these store types. For each respondent, therefore, store loyalty was calculated with respect to one of five product categories:

- personal care products
- leisure goods
- home furnishings
- clothing
- food/confectionery.

Consumers who had visited a particular department or mixed retail store without purchasing from any of these categories were not interviewed.

Thirdly, previous empirical studies have generally been based in one geographic location, such as the work carried out by Wrigley and Dunn in Cardiff. Doubtless there were sound methodological reasons for this narrow geographic focus, not least of which must have been the logistics of monitoring and recording behavioural data. Nevertheless, there is also a very strong case for drawing a sample from the national population to overcome any local factors that might disguise general trends. In an attempt to develop a nationally representative pattern of store loyalty, 750 consumers were interviewed across ten major sites in Britain. Managers at the main shopping centres in each of ten retail regions were identified and contacted. The final selection in each region was dependent upon their willingness to cooperate. In the event, seven of the shopping centres constituted the principal site in the region.

Each respondent was questioned about his/her shopping behaviour in connection with the store they had just exited, so each respondent was only questioned about one of five sectors. Twenty-two interviews were subsequently rejected because of poor cross-validation of interview data.

Our approach differed from previous studies which have mainly used diary panels as a means of data collection. Time, client and resource considerations, by necessity, guided our methodology. Whilst we relied on human memory for data accuracy, great attention was given to the questionnaire design to encourage accurate memory recall. The pilot fieldwork had indicated that accuracy of recall deteriorated over any timespan longer than one month. Cross-referencing was used throughout the questionnaire to validate individual answers and safeguard the data quality.

Part of the appeal of using the Enis-Paul Index as the measure of store loyalty lay in the fact that it was constructed around three separate inputs, each calculated from independent information collected during the interview which lasted approximately 15 minutes. Had a single measure been chosen, we would have become dependent on a small number of inputs and significantly increased the risk of inaccurate measurement.

Sampling of individual consumers was conducted on a quota basis; the quota specifications related to location, retail sector and socio-economic rating. Shoppers within the quota specifications were approached as they left stores. In all other respects, the survey comprised a representative cross-section of shoppers in their characteristics (sex, age, family size, working status) and shopping routines (interviews were conducted from Monday to Saturday and throughout the course of the day including during late night shopping). The main fieldwork was carried out in February 1992, once consumers had fallen back into their regular shopping patterns after Christmas and the January sales. Our findings from the data analysis stage are outlined below.

HOW LOYAL ARE CONSUMERS IN THE 1990S?

The Enis-Paul Index was calculated for each of the 728 survey respondents. The mean loyalty level of 'first choice' store was calculated to be 60.4 per cent with a standard deviation of 16.1 per cent. Like the original Enis-Paul study, our distribution of loyalty values approximate to a normal distribution, as Figure 2.3 shows. Therefore, we are able to confirm that the Enis-Paul Index can reasonably discriminate various degrees of store loyalty among shoppers.

It is interesting to make a brief comparison between the Enis-Paul results in 1970 and our own data. Their study of grocery retailing produced an average loyalty rating of 70.1 per cent and a standard deviation of 16.2 per cent, a remarkably similar spread of values to our own (sd = 16.1 per cent). At the disaggregate level, among the 161 shoppers in our study who were questioned about their grocery shopping behaviour, the average loyalty level to their 'first choice' food store was found to be 60.7 per cent.

However, it would be improper to make any categorical inferences from the comparison between the two studies since there are important methodological differences between research designs: Enis and Paul calculated store loyalty levels over a ten-week period from diary panel

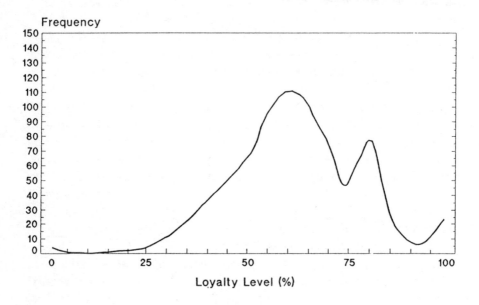

Figure 2.3 Frequency of customer loyalty values

data, whilst our ad hoc survey data recalled shopping behaviour over the previous four weeks. Further, previous research has found that store loyalty decreases over time (Wrigley and Dunn 1984b). They found an 11 per cent reduction in loyalty to grocery stores over a six-week period compared with their one-week measure and a 15 per cent difference over 24 weeks.

So, although their research suggests that the rate of loyalty decline stabilises, we can only surmise that were we to have measured store loyalty over the same time period as Enis and Paul, our average store loyalty figure would have been still lower, indicating an even wider temporal drift in loyalty behaviour.

Nonetheless, there is much circumstantial evidence to suggest that grocery shoppers in the 1990s in the UK are less loyal to their 'first choice' store than were their American counterparts in the 1960s. Despite the efforts by UK retail management to engender loyalty among their customers, greater choice of store, higher mobility levels and, perhaps, even the transition to impersonal self-service systems may have encouraged UK consumers to become more fickle and promiscuous in their shopping behaviour.

Are shoppers more loyal to stores in some retail sectors than others?

Whilst our study design prevented us from establishing whether *individuals* have differing loyalty profiles across retail sectors, we have been able to make comparisons across sectors at an *aggregate* level.

Our survey shows that store loyalty levels across the grocery, mixed retail and petrol sectors are very similar and do not vary significantly. However, both DIY and department stores do have significantly different scores from these three (Figure 2.4). Loyalty amongst consumers towards 'first choice' DIY stores is significantly lower than the other sectors. It would seem that retailers in this sector are struggling to gain any competitive advantage over one another, and failing to differentiate themselves.

We can suggest two primary reasons for this. Firstly, the 1970s' boom in the DIY trade encouraged rapid and widespread construction of DIY superstores, located in out-of-town developments with competitors clustered in close geographical proximity. This has generally minimised any significant site advantages from being established by any one retailer in this sector. Location has long been recognised as a key ingredient to retailing success and closely associated with repeat buying behaviour.

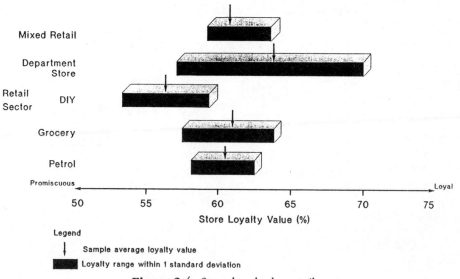

Figure 2.4 Store loyalty by retail sector

33

The absence of significant locational supremacy appears to have a dulling effect on consumer loyalty to individual DIY stores.

Secondly, DIY retailers seem to be failing to differentiate themselves on store image and perceived value. At interview, consumers commented that they were not usually conscious of which particular DIY store they were in; they all appeared to share very similar merchandising practices and failed to create individuality, so each store looked the same. On the evidence of the recent television advertising campaigns, DIY retailers seem content to compete on 'bleeding edge', price-slashing tactics, rather than creating a 'value added' proposition. On the evidence of our research, this approach fails to create strong loyalty ties with consumers. It remains to be seen if, in the longer term, the DIY chains are successful in their pioneering attempts at customer retention through loyalty cards.

In contrast, department stores attracted stronger loyalty amongst our respondents than any other retail sector. This finding is intuitively appealing since shopping in department stores has certain elitist and psycho-social qualities, rather like a 'lifestyle badge' that consumers are proud to wear. Interestingly, it was the one retail sector where respondents did not list location as being the driving force for choosing one department store in preference to others.

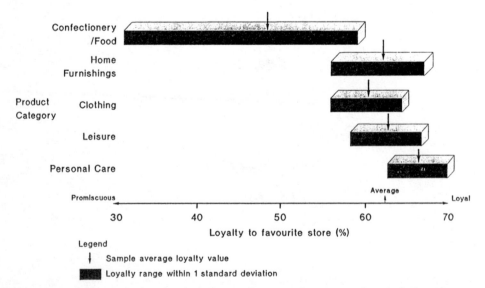

Figure 2.5 Store loyalty departmental or mixed store purchasing by product category

Re-analysing our database by product category *across* department and mixed retail stores shows that store loyalty levels do not differ markedly for clothing, leisure goods and home furnishings (Figure 2.5).

However, in the case of personal care products, respondents were noticeably more store loyal in their buying habits. Perhaps people tend to frequent the stores in which they know particular brands are sold or specialist advice can be sought. Whatever the root causes may be, personal care products seem to be a store loyalty generator amongst mixed retail and department stores. For those buying food/confectionery in mixed retail and department stores, loyalty to their 'first choice' was particularly low. However, there was noticeably more spread around the mean loyalty level. A possible explanation can be offered from unstructured customer responses during interviews: some bought food there as an occasional treat or as an emergency fall-back, but not as part of their regular routine. However, others favoured such stores as a matter of course, attracted as much by elitist values as the promise of quality brands. Other loyalties lay in between these dichotomous extremes.

In this section we have reaffirmed the value of the Enis-Paul Index as a means of measuring store loyalty and discriminating between consumers' shopping habits. We have demonstrated that store loyalty levels do differ between certain retail sectors and product categories. We have also shown that shoppers are particularly promiscuous in their buying habits from DIY stores and mixed retail/department stores when buying food. In contrast, loyalty to department stores is particularly high with regard to certain product categories, such as personal care products. Our main purpose has been to establish *whether* store loyalty levels do differ amongst retail sectors rather than to explain *why* levels might differ. Nevertheless, we have tried to offer plausible reasons for the behavioural differences where they have occurred.

ARE LOYAL SHOPPERS MORE PROFITABLE TO THE RETAILER?

In other industries, particularly in the services sector, a clear link has been made between the gearing effect of customer loyalty and account profitability, where modest improvements in customer retention can significantly improve business profitability (Reichhold and Sasser 1990; Buchanan and Gillies 1990).

In this study we have set out to establish whether similar conclusions can be reached in retailing. Given that the Enis-Paul Index includes a budget ratio input, we would expect loyal shoppers to spend *relatively* more of their budget (per cent) in their 'first choice' store than those less loyal. However, whether these consumers spend more in *absolute* terms (£) depends on the size of their £ budget (ie the total amount they have to spend across all stores or by store category). Previous studies have found that store loyalty is seemingly independent of the total amount consumers have to spend. However, in each case, these studies have been confined to the grocery sector (eg Cunningham 1961; Enis and Paul 1970). Dunn and Wrigley (1984) have expressed surprise at this finding and, like others in the past, have reasoned that one might expect store loyalty and total expenditure to be related.

Store loyalty and monthly spend

Contrary to these historical findings, we are able to report data which show for the first time an association between store loyalty and total allocated spend within a retail sector. Across the sample as a whole, the linear correlation coefficient is low ($r = -0.103$), but, nonetheless, statistically significant (at the 0.05 level). If the total sample is broken down into the five retail sectors, the same inverse association is found across four of the sectors, being strongest and most significant in mixed retail ($r = -0.295$) and DIY shopping ($r = -0.303$). Since the correlation coefficient is negative, it signifies that the higher a consumer's total monthly sector spend (£), the lower the level of loyalty attached to his/her 'first choice' store.

Importantly, however, we found the relationship to be *positive* and significant ($r = 0.239$) for grocery shopping, bucking the general trend found across the other sectors. So the greater the consumer's total monthly spend on groceries, the more loyal they are likely to be towards their 'first choice' store. This disparate association helps explain the relatively low negative correlation coefficient for the sample as a whole.

In order to explore how store loyalty and spend vary by shopping behaviour, we subdivided the sample into three loyalty bands each of which contained approximately equal numbers of respondents, as there were no natural break points in the distribution of loyalty values. We then designated the top third to be 'loyal' shoppers and the bottom third as 'promiscuous' and compared their monthly sector spends. We found that loyal shoppers have approximately 7 per cent *less* than average (across the sample of 728) to spend as compared to 13 per cent *more* for promiscuous shoppers (Figure 2.6). A T-test indicates the difference to be significant ($p = 0.05$).

When our data are disaggregated across retail sectors and product

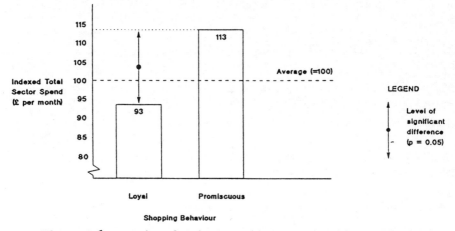

Figure 2.6 An index of sterling monthly sector spend for loyal and promiscuous shoppers

categories, this pattern is generally repeated; a significant difference in monthly spend (£) between loyal and promiscuous shoppers is found in all but petrol retailing where little difference was detected. This pattern of spend was found to be most noticeable for shoppers in mixed-retail stores where promiscuous shoppers spent three times as much as loyal shoppers each month.

In stark contrast to this general trend and in support of the findings from the correlation analysis, in grocery retailing loyal shoppers are found to spend significantly more per month than the promiscuous group. On average, they spend 50 per cent more on grocery products!

Store loyalty and budget allocation

Whilst we have shown that, generally, loyal shoppers tend to have smaller monthly budgets, by all expenditure-based measures of loyalty (including the Enis-Paul Index used in this research), we might expect loyal shoppers to spend proportionately *more* of their budget (per cent) than promiscuous shoppers in their 'first choice' store. Not only do we find this to be the case in our research, but we have also found that the degree of difference is surprisingly large, which reinforces Enis and Paul's observations of shopping behaviour in the 1960s. Across the two groups, loyal shoppers allocate over twice as much of their monthly budget (per cent) to their 'first choice' store than promiscuous shoppers, as Figure 2.7 indicates. Whilst the general trend is not unexpected, we were surprised at the magnitude of disparity.

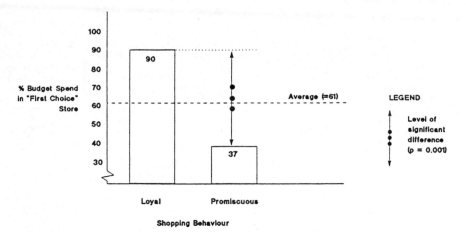

Figure 2.7 Proportion of sector monthly spend for loyal and promiscuous shoppers

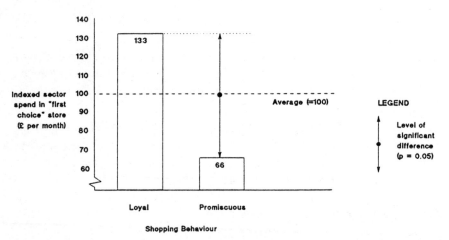

Figure 2.8 An index of sterling monthly spend in 'first choice' stores for loyal and promiscuous shoppers

This scale of difference was sustained across all five retail sectors and product categories without exception. So we have been able to establish that loyal shoppers tend to spend *less* in total (£) over the course of a month by sector (with the important exception of grocery store shopping), but allocate *more* of their budget (per cent) to their 'first choice' store. Combining these two contra-trends, we were able to conclude that loyal shoppers generally spend more per month in absolute terms (£) as well as relatively (per cent of budget allocated) in their 'first choice' stores (Figure 2.8).

Loyal shoppers tend to spend twice as much as promiscuous shoppers in their 'first choice' store.

This pattern holds true across the grocery, DIY and petrol retailing sectors, although, in the latter case, the directional trend is not statistically significant. At the product category level, the relationship is also consistent for personal care products, clothing and food/confectionery bought in department and mixed retail stores.

It is our belief that this finding is of great strategic importance to retailers in general and grocery retailers (and manufacturers) in particular, since in this case the loyalty benefit is further leveraged due to the fact that loyal shoppers tend to have larger grocery budgets than fellow shoppers in the first instance. This double leveraging effect in grocery retailing we have termed the double indemnity effect. It signifies that customers loyal to a particular grocery store tend to spend up to *four* times as much in their favourite store as promiscuous shoppers spend in their favourite stores.

IMPLICATIONS FOR RETAILERS

Although our findings are substantially more conclusive and broader ranging than those of the Enis-Paul study in certain respects, we are bound by the same observation which seems both timeless and acultural: loyal customers spend substantially more money in their favourite stores than do promiscuous shoppers. Furthermore, as these loyal customers are no more expensive to serve, we can realistically conclude that loyal customers are potentially more profitable to retailers. On the evidence of this research, retailers are fully justified in their recent attempts to increase customer loyalty in their stores. Quite how successful incentive schemes are in encouraging store loyalty is quite a separate issue and one which is beyond the scope of this chapter.

Since our study suggests that loyal customers are more profitable, retailers would benefit from developing their marketing strategy around the needs and wants of their loyal customers. Such a strategy would, nevertheless, only be of strategic interest if loyal customers comprise a substantial segment of the customer base, and if they share common traits to make them accessible beyond their in-store behaviour (for instance, socio-graphic characteristics and shopping protocols). In the absence of such an analysis, customer retention strategy is likely to be developed around loyalty programmes and frequent shopper promotions. Whilst both these tools are currently enjoying considerable interest at an operational level, the strategic approach to customer retention, based on differentiation through behavioural segmentation, remains limited.

CONCLUSIONS, LIMITATIONS AND NEW RESEARCH DIRECTIONS

In this chapter we have discussed two main issues arising from our empirical study of store loyalty and spend. Firstly, we have found that loyalty levels are surprisingly similar across a number of retail sectors and any top league retailer in the grocery, petrol or mixed retail sector can expect to enjoy a 60 per cent loyalty level across a composite measure of budget, patronage and switching factors. We conclude from comparisons with previous studies that store loyalty levels have fallen somewhat over the last 20 years and we highlight greater mobility, store choice and awareness as possible causes. The one sector to suffer from particularly low store loyalty levels is DIY retailing. DIY retail marketers are resorting to price discounting to try to secure competitive advantage on the one hand, whilst on the other, they are using loyalty schemes that are unlikely to be triggered solely on the basis of price cues.

The second issue addressed in this paper is the relationship between store loyalty and customer expenditure which our study identifies for the first time to be significantly associated. Thus, whilst we have found that loyal shoppers generally spend less in total per month (£) by sector than promiscuous customers, they do, however, spend more of it – about twice as much – in their 'first choice' store. This is particularly true in petrol and DIY retailing.

In grocery retailing, not only do loyal shoppers allocate proportionally more of their budget to their 'first choice' store (per cent), as in the other sectors, but they spend more on groceries (£) per se than their fellow shoppers. In practice the combined effect is that loyal shoppers can spend up to four times as much (£) in their 'first choice' store as their promiscuous counterparts. We have designated this anomaly the 'double indemnity' effect.

These loyalty-spend findings lead us to the inevitable conclusion that these customers represent the most profitable core of shoppers, a fact that has been established already in industry sectors outside retailing.

Our study clearly provides retailers with an incentive to reexamine ways in which to make loyal customers *more loyal* to their stores. The research imperatives must be, firstly, to explore the exact nature of the loyalty/profitability relationship, in order to appreciate the gearing effect on profitability that a marginal change in store loyalty can bring. Secondly, we must establish the means to access loyal customers *at the strategic level* to influence the 'first choice' decision, acting synergistically with loyalty programmes that operate at store level.

Whilst we are confident about the conclusions we have drawn, our work has raised more questions than it has answered and its limitations have to be recognised. Firstly, we have rather artificially designated the loyalty label without exploring salient determinants. Secondly, we have not addressed the temporal nature of loyalty. Loyalty seems to diminish over time, but the actual dynamics of store loyalty erosion remains completely unexplored here. Thirdly, we have not even begun to address individual consumer loyalty profiles across retail sectors, nor by site location. With regard to the first limitation cited, we believe that the data are significantly robust to warrant further analysis and, consequently, will be the subject of future communications. Both the other limitations we have mentioned highlight the frailty of our study and offer significant challenges to the research community.

Despite these limitations, we believe the paper makes a timely contribution to knowledge by underlining the importance of loyal customers in the retailing of fast-moving consumer goods and durables. It has been based on a substantial empirical study and brings attention to a subject that we believe will become the new battleground of retailing in the 1990s.

Enis-Paul Index Formula (Burford, Enis and Paul 1971)

The loyalty, L, of the ith (ie the 10th, 20th, etc) consumer towards a particular store is given in percentage form by:

$$L_i = 100 \left[b_i \times \frac{k+1-s_i}{m} \times \frac{n+1-p_i}{n} \right] \frac{1}{3}$$

where:

b_i = fraction of the budget for the product class allocated to the store during the survey period by the ith consumer

s_i = number of switches from the store to other stores during the survey period by the ith consumer

p_i = number of stores patronised by the ith consumer during the survey period

m = number of total store visits during the survey period

$k = m-1$ = number of opportunities to switch

n = number of stores available to the consumer to purchase product category goods during the survey period.

Acknowledgement

The authors would like to acknowledge financial support for the empirical study from Air Miles Travel Promotions Ltd.

References

Buchanan R and Gillies C (1990), 'Value managed relationships: the key to customer retention and profitability', *European Marketing Journal*, Vol 8 (4), pp 523–5.

Burford R L, Enis B M and Paul G W (1971), 'An index for the measurement of consumer loyalty', *Decision Sciences*, Vol 2, pp 17–24.

Carmen J M (1970), 'Correlates of brand loyalty; some positive results', *Journal of Marketing Research*, Vol 7, pp 67–76.

Charlton P (1973), 'A review of shop loyalty', *Journal of Market Research Society*, Vol 15, No 1, pp 35–51.

Chatfield C, Ehrenberg A S C and Goodhardt G J (1966), 'Progress on a simplified model of stationary purchasing behaviour', *Journal of the Royal Statistical Society*, Series A, 129, pp 317–67.

Christopher M, Payne A and Ballantyne D (1991), *Relationship Marketing: The Integration of Quality, Customer Service and Marketing*, Heinemann, London.

Crouchley R, Pickles A and Davies R D (1982a), 'Dynamic models of shopping behaviour: testing the linear learning model and some alternatives', *Geografiska Annaler* B, issue 64, pp 27–33.

—(1982b), 'A re-examination of Burnett's study of Markovian models of movement', *Geographical Analysis*, Vol 14, p 260.

Cunningham R M (1956), 'Brand loyalty – what, where, how much?', *Harvard Business Review*, Vol 34, Jan/Feb, p 116.

—(1961), 'Customer loyalty to store and brand', *Harvard Business Review*, Vol 40, Nov/Dec, pp 127–37.

de Chernatony L, Knox S D and Chedgey M (1992), 'Brand pricing in a recession', *European Journal of Marketing*, Vol 26, No 2, pp 5–14.

de Chernatony L and MacDonald M (1992), *Creating Powerful Brands*, Butterworth-Heinemann, Oxford.

Dunn R and Wrigley N (1984), 'Store loyalty for grocery products: an empirical study', *Area*, Vol 16, pp 307–14.

Ehrenberg A S C (1988), *Repeat Buying: Fact, Theory and Applications*, 2nd Edition, Oxford University Press, New York.

Ehrenberg A S C, Goodhardt G J and Barwise T P (1990), 'Double jeopardy revisited', *Journal of Marketing*, Vol 54, July, pp 82–91.

Enis B M and Paul G W (1970), 'Store loyalty as a basis for market segmentation', *Journal of Retailing*, Vol 46, No 3, pp 42–56.

Farley J V (1968), 'Dimensions of supermarket choice patterns', *Journal of Marketing Research*, Vol 5, pp 206–8.

Goodhardt G J, Ehrenberg A S C and Chatfield C (1984), 'The Dirichlet Model – a comprehensive model of buying behaviour', *Journal of the Royal Statistical Society*, Series A, 147, pp 621–55.

Jephcott J St G (1972), 'Consumer loyalty – a fresh look', *Proceedings of the 1972 Annual Conference*, Market Research Society, London.

Kau A K (1981), 'Patterns of Store Choice', Doctoral thesis London University.

Kau, A K and Ehrenberg A S C (1984), 'Patterns of store choice', *Journal of Marketing Research*, Vol XX1, pp 399–409.

Kelley R F (1967), 'Estimating ultimate performance levels of new retail outlets', *Journal of Marketing Research*, Vol 4, February, pp 13–19.

Knee D and Walters D (1985), *Strategy in Retailing: Theory and Application*, Philip Allan, Oxford.

Knox S D and de Chernatony L (1990), 'A buyer behaviour approach to merchandising and product strategy', *International Journal of Retailing and Distribution Management*, Vol 18, No 6, pp 21–30.

Knox S D and White H (1991), 'Retail buyers and their fresh produce suppliers: a power or dependency scenario?', *European Journal of Marketing*, Vol 25, No 1, pp 40–52.

Lamb T J and Goodhart G J (1989), 'A comparison of brand loyalty and store loyalty', *Working Paper No 93*, City University Business School, London.

Rao T R (1969), 'Consumers' purchase decision process: stochastic models', *Journal of Marketing Research*, Vol 6, pp 321–9.

Reichhold F F and Sasser W E Jr (1990), 'Zero defections: quality comes to services', *Harvard Business Review*, Sep–Oct, pp 105–11.

Richards J and Smiddy P (1985), 'The retail market – the non-property view', *Retail Report*, Healey and Baker, London.

Tate R S (1961), 'The supermarket battle for store loyalty', *Journal of Marketing*, Vol 25, pp 8–13.

Thompson B (1967), 'An analysis of supermarket shopping habits in Worcester, Massachusetts', *Journal of Retailing*, Vol 43, pp 17–29.

Wrigley N (1980), 'An approach to the modelling of shop-choice patterns: an exploratory analysis of purchasing patterns in a British city', in Herbert D T and Johnson R (eds) *Geography and the Urban Environment. Progress in Research and Applications*, Vol 3, Wiley, Chichester.

Wrigley N and Dunn R (1984a), 'Stochastic panel-data models of urban shopping behaviour: 1 Purchasing at individual stores in a single city', *Environment and Planning* A, Vol 16, pp 629–50.

—(1984b), 'Stochastic panel-data models of urban shopping behaviour: 2 Multi-store purchasing patterns and the Dirichlet model', *Environment and Planning A*, Vol 16, pp 759–78.

—(1984c), 'Stochastic panel-data models of urban shopping behaviour: 3 The interaction of store choice and brand choice', *Environment and Planning A,* Vol 16, pp 1, 221–1, 236.

—(1988), 'Models of store choice and market analysis' in Wrigley N (ed), *Patterns of Store Choice, Store Location and Market Analysis*, Routledge, London.

3

CONSUMERS' PERCEPTIONS OF MICRO-RETAIL LOCATION*

Gordon Foxall and Paul Hackett

OUTLINE

The basic principle of micro-retail design is that consumer mobility can be shaped such that specialist stores will be visited by shoppers en route to the anchor or attractor shops (eg departmental stores or large supermarkets) which they cannot avoid. The evidence for this proposition is piecemeal and anecdotal; it does not rest on accurate empirical observation of consumers' capacity to form mental maps of shopping areas and to find their way around them efficiently and effectively.

Environmental cognition – the mental configuration of the external physical context – has widespread implications for the ways in which citizens make sense of their locations and their consequent behaviour. Urban complexity impacts principally upon consumers: as public demand has imposed increasing pressure upon limited physical space in built-up areas, physically extensive, multiple-level developments have become so commonplace that multi-storey carparks, shopping developments and international airports are so familiar as to evoke little comment.

The *legibility* of the typical modern shopping mall – the ease with which it can be cognitively organised – may suffer compared with that of the more organically developed traditional shopping area: the pathways of the former tend to be of similar design and colouring, providing only the experienced shopper with cues as to which aisle they are traversing. Multi-level layouts add to the difficulties inherent in formulating accurate mental maps. Within a network of traditional high streets or a multi-aisled

* This chapter first appeared in *The International Review of Retail, Distribution and Consumer Research*, Vol 2, No 3, July 1992.

shopping precinct, nodes and landmarks are automatically provided at the intersections of roads or aisles.

In order to increase understanding of consumers' awareness of the relative positions of attractor versus specialist stores, studies are reported of their abilities to locate selected stores in two distinctive retail environments: a traditional, 'organic' high street shopping district and a modern, 'planned' out-of-town shopping centre. Three methods of assessing consumers' micro-retail locational perceptions and behaviour were employed: a wayfinding walk, a wayfinding commentary and a cognitive mapping exercise. Consumers' perceptions of micro-retail location corresponded only partially to the principles of shopping centre design. Respondents were differentially aware of primary and secondary attractor stores, as compared with specialists, in the planned shopping centre environment, but they were more aware of stores located at nodal and other prominent positions, regardless of their function, in the traditional high street environment.

INTRODUCTION

The essence of the out-of-town shopping centre is its having been deliberately designed, in contrast to the city centre shopping district which, by comparison, usually shows signs of having evolved organically. Describing the first as planned, the second as unplanned, overstates this difference but it is useful to call attention to the overall approach to design generally accorded new, suburban shopping centres as opposed to the necessarily more piecemeal design of urban shopping districts (Davies 1978; Jones 1989). One aspect of such planning involves comprehension of consumers' shopping behaviour at the micro-retail level, ie within the shopping area. Not only is this under-researched (Brown 1987): the assumed patterns of consumer mobility and motivation on which micro-retail design depends rely more on hearsay and causal observation than systematic investigation. This chapter outlines the principles on which micro-retail design is accomplished and the presumptions it makes with respect to consumer behaviour. It then reports the findings of studies of consumers' perceptions of, and wayfinding abilities in, two complex retail environments – a new out-of-town shopping centre and a high street shopping district in a traditional city – which raise questions for the understanding of how consumers mentally construe and achieve mobility within such contexts.

MICRO-RETAIL DESIGN AND CONSUMER BEHAVIOUR

The fundamental principle of micro-retail design is evident, from the structure of the earliest postwar shopping centre developments in the United States to the most sophisticated recent examples found on every continent. It is the juxtapositioning of 'anchor' stores, which attract buyers routinely and frequently, with specialist shops whose customers are believed to buy often on impulse, so that people are encouraged to notice and use the latter en route to or from the former (Beddington 1982; Darlow 1972; Johnson 1987; Sim and Way 1989).

At its simplest, this design includes a single mall, along which smaller tenants are positioned, at each end of which is a variety or department store (Gardner and Sheppard 1989). These larger, magnet or attractor stores need not be placed in the most accessible spots, for large numbers of consumers can be expected to seek them out in order to make indispensable purchases (eg of foodstuffs) or to compare merchandise with that on offer in similar stores elsewhere (Michell 1986; Scott 1989).

The attraction of suitable anchor tenants to shopping centres at their inauguration, and their subsequent retention, have therefore become central concerns of retail centre management. The so-called 'low impulse' trades they represent include not only department stores but, of increasing significance, large high-quality food supermarkets (Davies 1976; Davies and Rogers 1984; Dawson 1980, 1983; Dawson and Lord 1985).

At the other end of the spectrum, so-called 'high impulse' trades, which depend heavily on a continuous throughput of potential consumers, and which thus benefit from being located in prominent positions such as along malls and near the entrances to shopping centres, include jewellers, craft shops, clothes stores, photographic equipment specialists and florists. An intermediate group, 'secondary attractors', bring large num-bers of potential customers into contact with the specialist stores: they provide services that facilitate customer behaviour in one-stop retail developments, and they also employ large numbers of staff who make local purchases during breaks and on their way home. Banks and fast-food outlets obviously come into this category because of the essential consumer services they make available; other stores, such as pharmacies, that offer important non-impulse purchases also belong here, as do office buildings; and, perhaps less evidently, so do large bookshops and travel agencies which offer a change of pace and increase the overall variety of goods considered on a lengthy shopping trip.

This basic principle of design carries the implication that consumers' behaviour is susceptible to the 'cumulative attractiveness' of a variety of stores, and that the tenant mix of shopping centres should be actively managed to promote an optimum level of compatibility among the retailers (Nelson 1958). However, while the widespread advocacy of a planned arrangement of anchor and specialist stores is consistent with commonsense logic, evidence for it relies for the most part on casual observation and anecdote rather than a volume of dependable, systematic knowledge. Although groupings of potentially compatible retailers are frequently encountered, their propinquity may derive from the strictures of local planning regulations rather than their functional interdependence (eg Davies 1984). Evidence that consumers actually proceed from one type of store to another does not, of itself, establish that they thereby engage actively in comparative evaluations of merchandise, make more rational or more impulsive purchases, buy more or spend more. Moreover, even painstaking tracking of customer mobility has relied on observational methods which lack convincing monitoring and recording techniques or on the retrospective self-reports of consumers (Brown 1987).

Although the patterns of consumers' mobility and motivation assumed by the principles of micro-retail design and tenant mix management are supported by commonsense logic and limited observation, systematic evidence for the underlying proposition that consumers perceive complex retail environments in ways compatible with the theory has not been produced. What evidence there is comes mainly from consultants' reports and retailers' informal accounts of their locational experience and aspirations rather than in the form of the reliable, theoretically derived results of replicated research. An informative exception is the survey evidence presented by Brown (1987) for retailers' perceptions of micro-retail location and their beliefs about its implications for customer behaviour and trade. This confirms a tripartite classification of stores: the anchors that generate trade by providing opportunities for comparison of merchandise and perceptible value-for-money (variety and department stores and, increasingly, large-scale grocery retailers); secondary generators, notably service organisations that act as catalysts to general purchasing (banks, restaurants, fast-food cafés, estate agents, travel firms etc); and the specialists that provide personal products and services (opticians, clothiers, gift shops etc).

The respondents to Brown's survey confirmed the pre-eminent position of the first category, the magnet stores on which the attraction of business in general crucially depends. They drew special attention to the generative effect on trade of the secondary attractors whose impact was deemed to be strong and growing. In addition, the respondents claimed there was a tendency towards intra-trade consumer behaviour – going from one clothier to another, one food store to another, and so on. Inter-trade linkages were also believed to be important: despite the belief that shopping for convenience goods occurs independently of that for comparison goods, the implication of the survey is that these modes of consumer behaviour coexist as routine purchasing gives an opportunity to gather information on a continuous basis about infrequently purchased durable products (cf Wilkie and Dickson 1991). Finally, the surveyed retailers expressed consistent preferences for being located close to food stores, department stores, variety stores, restaurants, banks, and their own direct competitors.

Although these results are derived from a city centre shopping location, Belfast, which presents atypical circumstances for consumers, they have been described in some detail on account of their consistency with several assumptions underlying the revealed principles of micro-retail design. Their significance lies in their annunciation of belief in inter-store compatibility, tenant mix optimisation, and the resulting cumulative attraction by individuals directly involved in the outcomes of micro-retail design. However, this chapter's study, like others, is necessarily limited by its dependence upon self-reports, perceptions and impressions that may not be accurate and reliable and which cannot be consistently linked to objective measures of inter-store sales synergy. To expect this would be to go beyond the scope and purpose of the investigation; nevertheless, the assumptions about consumer behaviour on which these beliefs stand are no more surely established than before.

A RESEARCH PERSPECTIVE

There is a need for a broader, systematic examination of the nature of consumer mobility and buying patterns in complex retail settings. Reliable evidence is especially lacking that would substantiate the widespread belief in a synergistic interaction resulting from consumers' opportunities to visit a variety of stores located in close proximity, either in terms of higher sales for the retailers, or a more satisfying range of purchases for the consumer. This is not to overlook the obvious convenience for consumers of one-stop shopping, or to assert in the absence of evidence that the patterns of behaviour assumed by micro-retail locational designers, retailers and retailing academics are necessarily inaccurate. But it is necessary to point out the relatively flimsy evidence upon which many prevalent beliefs rest and to question whether there exists an achievable optimal tenant mix that will generate higher spending than would otherwise occur.

Micro-retail theory appears to rest on simplistic notions of consumer behaviour and its cognitive and perceptual determinants and a failure to consider alternative, equally plausible patterns of movement and store choice. The designation 'impulse trades', for instance, is misleading since it invites neglect of the fact that many, if not all, the corresponding purchases would have been made, perhaps at some other time and place: at most it is the 'here and now' of such purchases that can be influenced by the proximity of the shops in question. There is no evidence that consumers who currently need the services of opticians, clothiers and gift shops will not assiduously seek them out (though, admittedly, there will usually be far fewer such customers than those who can be expected to find supermarkets and department/variety stores), nor that organic purchases made at these and other specialist shops while the customer is en route to or from anchor stores are additional to their spending on the items they retail.

One of the reasons for the lack of evidence for this theory is the methodological difficulty of conducting sound empirical research in so complicated an area of human behaviour. It is possible, however, to take straightforward measures of the relative ease with which consumers are able to find their way around planned versus organic shopping areas, and of the elements of micro-retail design most frequently and accurately perceived by consumers. The results of such comparatively simple investigations, while not answering all the difficulties mentioned above, should establish whether the hierarchy of primary and secondary attractors, and specialist stores assumed by the locational literature, is reflected in consumers' cognitive perspective of shopping centres and other retail developments. Such measures would include the practical accuracy of consumers' wayfinding in traditional and modern complex retail environments, and of their attempts to pinpoint the location of specified stores, primary and secondary attractors and specialist stores, on an outline map of the retail area.

Cognitive mapping

The traditional high street and the modern shopping centre pose different problems of complexity. The shopping centre, containing pathways of similar design and colouring, may provide consumers with fewer definitive cues as to their current location; yet the organically developed shopping district can be rambling and illogical. The multi-level layout of many shopping centres may make wayfinding problematic; but organic shopping districts contain multi-storey shops arranged along pathways of differing gradients. Cognitive mapping, by monitoring the ways in which people process and apply information about the physical environment, presents a method by which the effects of these complex retail environments on consumer wayfinding might be compared (Canter 1977; Chase and Chi 1981; Evans 1980; Golledge 1987; Kaplan and Kaplan 1982; Lynch 1960; Moore 1979; Saarinen 1976; Stea 1974). Cognitive mapping by consumers has been the subject of several studies in which cognitive distance, among other variables, has been identified as determinative of consumers' store selection (Cadwallader 1975, 1981; Golledge and Rushton 1976; Mackay, Olshavsky and Sentell 1975; Sommer and Aitken 1982).

Cognitive mapping can contribute specifically to the present debate by establishing the extent to which a planned shopping centre is legible to consumers – ie to whom it is easily cognitively organised. Five separate components of legibility have been distinguished (Lynch 1960): *paths* (routes along which people travel), *edges* (non-travelled lines such as cliffs, and the boundaries of rivers or oceans), *districts* (medium-sized city areas identified by residents as having a specific character), *nodes* (well-known points travelled to and from, often important junctures of paths at crossroads or squares), and *landmarks* (features which are easily seen and memorable due to their large size, or if small, their uniqueness).

Research questions and design

The research was intended to answer two particular questions. First, is consumer wayfinding more successful in the modern, suburban planned shopping centre or the organic, traditional high street shopping district? And, second, what features of the retail environment comprise the cognitive maps used by consumers as they navigate these shopping areas: the functionally defined attractor and specialist stores, or stores which, regardless of their function, are prominent for their being positioned at nodes, or because they constitute or are near landmarks or boundaries?

Three empirical investigations are described below. First, a 'wayfinding walk' was undertaken in which consumers in both a planned and an organic shopping environment demonstrated their ability to walk without deviation to a randomly selected, named store. Secondly, consumers were asked, again in each retail context, to give a 'wayfinding commentary' by verbally describing the most economic route from their current position to a named store. Finally, consumers in each location were asked to pinpoint the map location of several designated stores including those which would, according to the literature reviewed above, be classified as primary attractors, secondary attractors and specialists.

The last exercise was based on three lines of reasoning derived from micro-retail location theory. First, if department and variety stores, and supermarkets indeed, act as anchors, magnets, or attractors, their positions within shopping environments should be accurately identified by consumers most often of all the three types of store. Their indispensability to the consumer, arising from the opportunities for comparative evaluation they offer, the value-for-money they provide, and their having been purposefully sought out despite their non-prime locations, should make them the most memorable stores. Secondly, the specialist stores, which are multiply represented by competing outlets in most complex shopping environments and which, according to revealed micro-retail design principles, rely on consumers' visits to other stores rather than their own individuality and uniqueness of identity, should be the least memorable in terms of location and, therefore, the least accurately pinpointed. Thirdly, between these extremes, the secondary attractors should stand out as memorable and capable of being positioned on a map with greater accuracy than specialist stores but less accuracy than variety and department stores and supermarkets.

METHODOLOGY

Locations

The design principles discussed above have been most frequently applied in planned out-of-town/suburban shopping centres. Consumers' perceptions of the micro-location of retail outlets might, however, differ in organic, traditional high street shopping districts from their perceptions of retail micro-location in these planned environments. The research therefore provides a comparison of both types of shopping environment. Of the locations investigated, the retail shopping centre represents a relatively new building development in Britain, often involving an extended built environment on more than one level, while the high street shop setting represents a traditional retail location in which the entrances to stores at least are found universally at ground level. While the selected examples are both of rather small dimension (approximately 1 sq km), they are geographically complex physical areas in terms both of the changes in direction which routes around them make necessary and the relative spacing between places and features.

The urban shopping district location chosen was at Worcester, a traditional city in the English Midlands. The city is over a thousand years old and contains several features within and adjacent to the centre which were constructed several hundred years ago – a cathedral, parish churches, shops, public houses etc. The shopping area comprises an asymmetrical network of pedestrian streets. A number of alleys and smaller streets run between the major thoroughfares. Several newer shop units and shopping squares complement the historical development.

Parts of the suburban shopping centre chosen for this study, Merry Hill in the Black Country, which was constructed in the 1980s, have been open for over five years while adjacent areas are still under development (Brown 1990). The building consists of a series of asymmetrically linking corridors, none of which constitutes the 'main' corridor; nor does any of the intersections provide the centre's focal point. Stores are of varying sizes and are sited on both storeys; some of the larger stores occupy positions on both levels, one above the other. Within this layout, containing interchanges and corridors which appear very similar to each other, it is comparatively easy to become disorientated.

Procedure

The research was conducted during March and April when neither venue would attract a disproportionate number of tourists. Two researchers/interviewers, one male and one female, undertook the empirical investigations, for twelve days in a period of two weeks (including Saturdays but not Sundays). All periods of the day, during shop opening hours, were covered by the survey, which employed starting points selected randomly throughout the shopping areas. Higher response rates were apparent at the shopping centre where it was easier to approach customers and to find convenient locations in which to conduct the interviews. Separate samples were recruited for each of the three studies so that experience of the shopping area engendered by one study did not contaminate another. Respondents in the wayfinding walk and the following commentary studies were asked to locate only one store, compared with potentially up to 24 in the mapping study, because the very nature of the exercise would encourage them mentally to place the additional stores used as cues, which would have contaminated further attempts at locating units.

Wayfinding walk

This study was undertaken in order to investigate further wayfinding abilities of consumers within retail settings. Potential respondents were approached at points peripheral to the mapping area and asked to walk with the interviewer to specified shops. The shops, all chosen by the researchers, were selected in pseudo-random fashion from the official maps of the shopping areas. The selection involved shops which were not visible to the respondents at the starting point and which required subjects to make a change in direction. In addition, within the shopping centre, target stores were nominated which required subjects to make changes between floor levels.

Members of the resulting opportunity samples of 24 respondents in the high street and 40 in the shopping centre were asked to take the shortest route of which they were aware to the specified target shop. If a respondent stated that they were unable to walk to the named store, this was noted and a second (third or fourth as necessary) was nominated. Subjects were accompanied on their task by an interviewer who walked slightly behind the subject in order not to cue the direction taken. The route taken was recorded by the interviewer on a map of the shopping district.

Wayfinding commentary

This study investigated respondents' ability to describe verbally the location of specified high street/shopping centre stores and their preferred route to each. The methodology was similar to that used for the wayfinding walk with the exception that, instead of being asked to walk with the interviewer to the nominated target, respondents were required to describe the shortest route to the target. Thirty-five consumers participated in the high street study; 52 in the shopping centre. Target shops were chosen as in the preceding study; once again, none was visible from the starting point and the location of each required changes in both direction and level. Additional stores were nominated when the subject reported being unable to describe the route to the first named. The route described by the respondent was recorded by the interviewer on a map visible only to him/herself.

Objective mapping

Maps were prepared showing, respectively, the city centre shopping district with all its retail units and pathways, each store individually numbered, and the upper and lower malls of the shopping centre, again detailing each of the retail units, each of which was identified only by a

Figure 3.1 Worcester: the high street shopping district

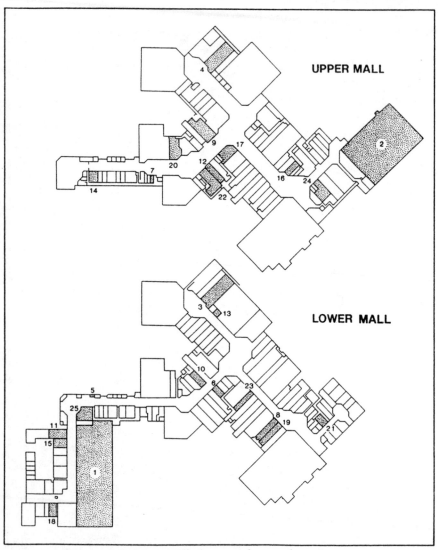

Figure 3.2 Merry Hill: the out-of-town shopping centre

number; neither of the maps, shown in Figures 3.1 and 3.2 omitting non-target stores, contained other information which would be useful in locating stores.

The approach chosen to assess cognitive mapping abilities within the high street shopping district required consumers to identify a series of specified shops on the prepared map of the location (Figure 3.1). Twenty-four shops were then chosen from the 264 recorded on an official map of the city to include attractor, secondary attractor and specialist stores. The identities and locations of these organisations listed on an official map of the city as trading out of each of the chosen units were confirmed. A similar procedure was followed in the case of the shopping centre: 24 shop units were selected from the 177 shown on the official map of the centre; the identity of the selected stores was again checked (Figure 3.2).

The target stores were dispersed over the area of the city's central shopping district and throughout the two-storey shopping centre. In both cases, the selected retail units included stores classified broadly on the basis of the research reviewed above as anchor stores, secondary attractors and specialists. Although some prior research has identified food supermarkets as secondary attractors, their importance as anchor locations is evident from the work of Brown (1987) and these retail outlets were, therefore, included in the anchor category. As far as possible, similar assortments of stores were selected for the two locations to facilitate comparisons; however, where the retail mix of one or other centre contained a unique tenant (such as the tourist information centre at Worcester), this was included.

Three anchor stores were chosen in Worcester city centre: a supermarket (Sainsbury's) and two rather different department/variety stores (Littlewoods and W H Smith). The retail mix at the Merry Hill shopping centre necessitated a rather different selection of anchor stores: two supermarkets (Asda and Sainsbury's) and a variety store (W H Smith). The W H Smith stores were chosen to reflect the role of the upper and lower malls at Merry Hill, and the twin outlets, one door apart at Worcester. Five secondary attractors were chosen in the high street shopping district: the tourist information centre, a public utility (the Midland Electricity Board showroom), a travel agent (Lunn Poly), a café-bar, and the National Westminster Bank. Only three secondary attractors were included at Merry Hill: the Midland Bank, the Post Office and a public utility (the British Gas showroom). No café was included in the latter selection of target stores since at Merry Hill most cafés and restaurants are located in a single wing of the upper mall; respondent confusion might have contaminated the results if one of these was selected at random. Finally, a range of specialist stores was included at each location (detailed in Tables 3.2 and 3.3 pp 60 and 61), selected as far as possible to be comparable.

Respondents were shoppers approached by one of two researchers, one male, one female, within the city and asked to participate. Each respondent was shown the map and the list of shops and asked to supply a unit number from the map for each of 24 selected stores. In the high street, 57 consumers so recruited into an opportunity sample completed the procedure. At no time were members of the sample provided with the names of roads, churches or other physical features present on the map; nor were verbal assistance, criticism or reinforcement provided. The interviews were conducted in locations from which none of the target stores was visible. The research design adopted in the shopping centre was identical to that used in the high street location in order to facilitate comparison of the results: each of 123 respondents participated in the location of the 24 target shops on a prepared map.

RESULTS

Wayfinding walk

Of the 24 high street subjects, 16 (67 per cent) were able to walk to the nominated shop; 7 could not walk towards a nominated store, and one could not complete the exercise. Three of the successful high street subjects made mistakes of direction, minor deviations in each case. In performing this task in the shopping centre, 32 (80 per cent) of the 40 respondents were able to walk directly to a nominated shop, although this was sometimes not the first named. The routes required changes in horizontal and vertical direction. Moreover, all these respondents took what was the most direct route to the store in question.

Wayfinding commentary

Of the 35 subjects who participated in the high street study, 20 (57 per cent) produced a perfect performance. Fifteen shops were unknown to subjects, these being their first, second or third nominated shop. Five errors were made by three subjects all of whom went on to fail to complete their commentary; all these errors were misjudgements about the appropriate junction at which to make turns. In the shopping centre, 40 (77 per cent) of the 52 subjects completed the direction commentary to their specified target shop without mistake. Of the ten errors committed six were in the horizontal plane and four involved a choice of the incorrect floor.

Objective mapping

In the high street location, the number of shops correctly identified and perfectly positioned on the map was 6.61 (standard deviation = 4.25). For the shopping centre, the mean number of correctly identified stores was 4.45 (sd = 3.79). The difference between the mean numbers of stores identified with total accuracy in the two studies is significant: t = 3.55, p<.002, two-tailed test.

Table 3.1 summarises the results of the three studies. The frequencies with which the target stores were correctly identified are shown in Tables 3.2 and 3.3. The patterns of consumers' perceptions apparent from these tables support the revealed principles of micro-retail location in only a general way; although a broad hierarchy can be identified, there are several important anomalies.

Table 3.1 Summary of results

	High street shopping district	Out-of-town shopping centre
Wayfinding walk Number of respondents making accurate location[1]	16 (67%)	32 (80%)
Wayfinding commentary Number of respondents making accurate location[1]	16 (67%)	40 (77%)
Mapping exercise Mean number of accurate locations[2]	6.61 (4.25%)	4.45 (3.79%)

[1] Percentage shown in brackets
[2] Standard deviations shown in brackets

In the high street shopping district at Worcester, the outlet which was most often correctly identified was an anchor store, the Sainsbury supermarket, but the other anchor stores are ranked sixth (W H Smith, which has two almost adjacent shopfronts) and eighth (Littlewoods department store). The tourist information office, a secondary attractor, holds the third position. Several specialist shops intervene among these: HMV (records), Paplows (jewellers), and Wallis (women's fashions), Elts (shoes) and Sharpes (bedrooms). A significant anomaly from the micro-retail design perspective is the appearance of two secondary attractors at the sixteenth and seventeenth positions in Table 3.2: the Conservatory café-bar and the National Westminster Bank. Finally, the last seven places in the list are occupied by specialist stores, most of which have rather small frequencies of correct location indicating their need of strong attractor stores to draw consumers to them.

Table 3.2 Proportion of respondents accurately locating each
store in high street mapping exercise

Store	Map identification number	Percentage correct
Sainsbury (supermarklet)	2	77
HMV (records)	20	58
Tourist Information	25	54
Paplows (jewellers)	14	53
Wallis (clothes)	8	49
WH Smith (variety)	3, 4	42
Elts (shoes)	11	37
Littlewoods (departmental)	1	36
MEB (electricity board showroom)	24	33
Sharpes (bedrooms)	18	33
Lunn Poly (travel agent)	23	28
SPCK (bookshop)	15	23
Country Casuals (clothes)	6	21
Sportsco	22	17
Gemmas Craft Shop	13	16
Conservatory café-bar	17	16
National Westminster Bank	21	12
Curtess (shoes)	12	9
Eyeland Express (optician)	16	9
Zebra Fashions	5	5
Foxy Lady (clothes)	7	5
Foster (menswear)	9	5
Austin Reed (menswear)	10	5
Our Price (records)	18	0

The eleven high street stores most frequently correctly identified have in
common that they occupy nodal positions: they include three secondary
attractors and five specialist shops, all shops prominently placed at
intersections of streets, one large supermarket positioned at the end of a
long walkway, a large department store, and a two-fronted variety store.
The single most frequently identified building, the largest supermarket
within the city centre, was also a landmark. The store ranked at number
twelve in Table 3.2, the specialist SPCK bookshop, is positioned near a
prominent landmark, a statue of Sir Edward Elgar. Those target units
which were least often correctly identified were positioned midway along
the pathways; since they did not constitute important points of reference,
their locations were presumably less firmly fixed within consumers'
perceptual frames and they were thus most often misplaced.

Table 3.3   Proportion of respondents accurately locating each store in shopping centre mapping exercise

Store	Map identification number	Percentage correct
Asda (supermarket)	1	66
Laura Ashley (clothes, fabrics, furnishings)	17	57
Sainsbury (supermarket)	2	47
WH Smith (variety)	3, 4	29
Barratt (shoes)	11	24
Burton (menswear)	9	19
Midland Bank	21	18
British Gas	24	15
Wallis (clothes)	8	13
Sharpes (bedrooms)	18	13
Post Office	25	13
Woolworths Music and Video	20	13
Watchbox (jewellers)	14	12
Torq (jewellers)	13	11
Our Price (records)	19	11
Country Casuals (clothes)	6	7
First Sight (opticians)	15	7
Astral Sport	22	7
Olympus Sport	23	7
Bodyline/Flirtz (clothes)	5	6
Cecil Gee (clothes)	10	6
Olivers (shoes)	12	4
Special Eyes (opticians)	16	2
Ondine (clothes)	7	0

In the shopping centre at Merry Hill, anchor stores occupy three of the top four rankings in terms of frequency of accurate identification (Table 3.3): these are the Asda and Sainsbury supermarkets and the W H Smith variety store which is located on two levels of the centre. Intervening among them in second place is the Laura Ashley (clothes, fabrics and furnishings) store which occupies a particularly prominent nodal position. The three secondary attractors occupy the seventh, eighth and eleventh placings: Midland Bank, British Gas and the Post Office. However, several specialist shops intervene among the anchors and secondary attractors: in addition to Laura Ashley, these are Barratt's (shoes), Burton (menswear), Wallis (women's fashions), and Sharpes (bedrooms). In this instance, these 'anomalous' stores, with the exception of Laura Ashley, do not appear to be placed so obviously at nodes or close to landmarks. The last thirteen positions in Table 3.3 are all occupied by specialist stores.

While Barratt's (shoes) and the Post Office, which appear relatively high in the ranking shown in Table 3.3, are located at nodes, several other shops which appear at nodal locations were only infrequently located: these are Special Eyes (opticians), Watchbox (jewellery) and Woolworths Music and Video.

DISCUSSION

Performances in both the wayfinding walks and commentaries were considerably better within the shopping centre location than the high street. Moreover, judged by the proportion of respondents providing correct answers, location-finding performance was more accurate in the wayfinding walk condition, regardless of location, than in the commentary condition. In both of these exercises, consumers' ability to locate stores selected by the interviewer puts the relatively poor performances of consumers in the mapping study into context. It appears that respondents were employing different cognitive skills or processes in the more abstract mapping exercise from the more active procedures used in the later studies. The sequencing of landmarks is an important ability in the wayfinding task (Cousins et al 1983; Waller 1986) and subjects were apparently well able to accomplish this task. The results indicate that walking through the location, and even just imagining doing so, more readily accessed the sequential nature of environmental features than did the more basic shop location recall attempts requiring recall of the spatial positioning of stores which are experienced in a three-dimensional space and their representation on a two-dimensional map. Moreover, while in the mapping study high street respondents produced better results than those in the shopping centre this was reversed in the two later studies.

In the organic context of the high street shopping district, consumers' accuracy in locating target stores appears to rest on their occupying nodal or landmark positions or being found adjacent to landmarks. However, the relatively low levels of accurate identification recorded for the National Westminster Bank and Conservatory café-bar, both of which were located close to the Sainsbury's supermarket, suggests that primary attractors may have little drawing power for secondary attractors which exercise this role if at all in their own right. This is not entirely overridden in the case of the shopping centre location, as witness the importance of the Laura Ashley and Barratt positions, but there is rather more emphasis on the functional import of the stores accurately identified with greater frequency. They are in less need of being sited at nodes; being so sited appears to have no consistent influence over consumers' locational accuracy. Nor were the best identified stores in the shopping centre those centrally positioned or on the lower mall which has more entrances than the upper and to which the bus terminus is directly linked.

Consumers appear to be employing different approaches to cognitive mapping in the two environments and, we would presume on the basis of the wayfinding exercises, to be influenced in their movements around the respective shopping areas by different factors. In the high street shopping district, respondents identified shops positioned around nodes, and close to landmarks, some of which were large attractor stores such as a supermarket. In the out-of-town shopping centre, while again using supermarkets as landmarks, they did not identify shops around nodal positions more frequently than other shops; their perceptual behaviour, as manifested in their cognitive mapping and wayfinding abilities, suggests that their consumer behaviour was more in line with that predictable from the principles of shopping centre design. Moreover, the recognition of secondary attractors, service organisations such as banks and travel agencies, was consistent with shopping centre design principles in the out-of-town shopping centre but not in the shopping district of the traditional city.

It is, perhaps, understandable that in the context of the planned shopping centre, consumer behaviour appears more sensitive to the physical features that would result from the implementation of micro-retail design principles and would remember the positions of attractor and secondary attractor stores on the whole better than those of specialist stores. It is also understandable that in the relatively organic context of the high street shopping district, they would be guided to a greater extent by both retail and non-retail physical features of the environment and that prominence of positioning at these places may be of greater importance to retailers than the propinquity of anchor stores. The results, therefore, lead us to question the assumption that consumer behaviour is necessarily influenced by the attractor/specialist store relationship attempted in modern shopping centres. The evidence that we have presented indicates that traditional, relatively organic shopping district layouts also permit consumers to perceive clearly the stores they require and to navigate among them effectively, though apparently using different landmarks from those on which contemporary retail planning is founded.

REFERENCES

Beddington N (1982), *Design for Shopping Centres*, Butterworth, London.

Breheny M J (1988), 'Practical methods of retail location analysis: a review', in Wrigley N (ed) *Store Choice. Store Location and Market Analysis*, Routledge, London.

Brown S (1987), 'Retailers and micro-retail location: a perceptual perspective', *International Journal of Retailing*, 2(3), pp 3–21.

—(1990), 'The retail park: customer usage and perceptions of a retailing innovation', *Service Industries Journal*, 10, pp 364–76.

Cadwallader M (1975), 'A behavioural model of spatial decision making', *Economic Geography*, 51, pp 339–49.

—(1981), 'Towards a cognitive gravity model: the case of consumer spatial behaviour', *Regional Studies*, 15, pp 175–84.

Canter D (1977), *The Psychology of Place*, Architectural Press, London.

Chase W G and Chi, M T H (1981), 'Cognitive skill: implications for spatial skill in large scale environments', in J H Harvey (ed) *Cognition, Social Behavior and the Environment*, Erlbaum, New Jersey.

Cousins J H, Siegal A W and Maxwell E E (1983), 'Wayfinding and cognitive mapping in large scale environments: a test of a developmental model', *Journal of Experimental Child Psychology*, 35, pp 1–20.

Darlow C (ed) (1972), *Enclosed Shopping Centres*, Architectural Press, London.

Davies R L (1976), *Marketing Geography: with special reference to retailing*. Retailing and Planning Associates, Corbridge.

—(1978) 'Issues in retailing', in Hall P (ed), *Issues in Urban Society*, Penguin, Harmondsworth.

—(1984), *Retail and Commercial Planning*, Croom Helm, London.

Davies R L and Rogers D S (eds) (1984), *Store Location and Store Assessment Research*, Wiley, Chichester.

Dawson J A (ed) (1980), *Retail Geography*, Croom Helm, London.

—(1983), *Shopping Centre Development*, Longman, London.

Dawson J A and Lord J D (eds) (1985), *Shopping Centre Development: Policies and Prospects*, Croom Helm, London.

Evans G W (1980), 'Environmental cognition', *Psychological Bulletin*, 88, pp 259—287.

Foxall G R and Goldsmith R E (1994), *Consumer Psychology for Marketing Managers*, Routledge, London.

Gardner C and Sheppard J (1989), *Consuming Passion: The Rise of Retail Culture*, Unwin Hyman, London.

Golledge R G (1987), 'Environmental cognition', in Stokols D and Altman I (eds), *Handbook of Environmental Psychology*, Vol 1, Wiley, Chichester.

Golledge R G and Rushton G (eds) (1976), *Spatial Choice and Spatial Behavior: Geographic Essays on the Analysis of Preferences and Perceptions*, Ohio State University Press, Columbus, OH.

Hackett P, Foxall G R and Van Raaij F (1993), 'Consumers in retail environments', in Gärling T and Golledge R G (eds), *Behavior and Environment: Psychological and Geographical Approaches*, North-Holland, Amsterdam.

Johnson D B (1987), 'The West Edmonton Mall – from super-regional to mega-regional shopping centre', *International Journal of Retailing*, 2(2), pp 53–69.

Jones K and Simmons J (1990), *The Retail Environment*, Routledge, London.

Jones P (1989), 'The modernisation and expansion of central shopping centres', *Service Industries Journal*, 9, pp 399–405.

Kaplan S and Kaplan R (1982), *Cognition and Environment*, Prager, New York.

Lynch K (1960), *The Image of the City*, MIT Press, Cambridge, MA.

Mackay D B, Olshavsky R W and Sentell G (1975), 'Cognitive maps and spatial behavior of consumers', *Geographical Analysis*, 7, pp 19–34.

Michell G (1986), *Design in the High Street*, Architectural Press, London.

Moore G T (1979), 'Knowing about environmental knowing: the current state of theory and research on environmental cognition', *Environment and Behavior*, 11, pp 33–70.

Nelson R L (1958), *The Selection of Retail Locations*, Dodge, New York.

Saarinen T (1976), *Environmental Planning: Perception and Behavior*, Houghton Mifflin, Boston, MA.

Scott N K (1989), *Shopping Centre Design*, Von Nostrand Reinhold, London.

Sim L L and Way C R (1989), 'Tenant placement in a Singapore shopping centre', *International Journal of Retailing*, 4(3), pp 4–16.

Sommer R and Aitken S (1982), 'Mental mapping of two supermarkets', *Journal of Consumer Research*, 9, pp 211–15.

Stea D (1974), 'Architecture in the head: cognitive mapping', in Lang J, Burnette

C, Moleski W and Vachon D (eds), *Designing for Human Behavior*, Dowden, Hutchinson and Ross, Stroudsberg, PA.

Waller G (1986), 'The development of route knowledge: multiple dimensions', *Journal of Environmental Psychology*, 6, pp 109–19.

Wilkie W L and Dickson P R (1991), 'Shopping for appliances: consumers' strategies and patterns of information search', in Kassarjian H H and Robertson T S (eds), *Perspectives in Consumer Behavior*, Prentice-Hall, Englewood Cliffs, NJ.

4

A BUYER BEHAVIOUR APPROACH TO MERCHANDISING AND PRODUCT POLICY*

Simon Knox

OUTLINE

During the last decade, continental cheese manufacturers have successfully penetrated the UK market. Sales of their products now account for 12 per cent of the total cheese market. As the penetration and consumption of continental cheeses has continually increased, there has been a general decline in sales of traditional British cheeses such as Cheddar and Cheshire. Given the conditions surrounding the development of a Single European Market, continental manufacturers are likely to increase their marketing activities in the UK since there is still considerable volume potential; UK cheese consumption per capita is currently half the level of consumers in mainland Europe. These manufacturers have been very quick to recognise the importance of UK major multiple retailers, both as change agents in the market channel and in providing market access through direct delivery. The top five multiples sell two-thirds of all the continental cheeses bought in this country. Their own-label product ranges account for over half the continental cheeses stocked and, in the absence of sustained advertising by the manufacturers of brands, further growth in the sector will be dependent upon the multiples stocking an extensive range, with an implicit reliance on point-of-purchase impact to facilitate sales.

This chapter describes exploratory research amongst continental cheese buyers designed to determine the level of influence (and the degree of interaction) which product and in-store purchase situation have upon their purchasing decisions. Through the process of discriminating between the behaviours of frequent and occasional purchasers using

---

* This paper first appeared in the *International Journal of Retail and Distribution Management*, Vol 18, No 6, 1990 © MCB University Press Ltd.

Belk's model (1975) and a research protocol based upon Iyer's application of script behaviour in-store (1989), a very clear picture of the saliency
of both product and situational factors emerged.

Frequent purchasers of continental cheeses tended to have a wider
choice set of brands and own-labels which could be influenced by staff
advice and could lead to the possibility of unplanned purchases.
Occasional purchasers, on the other hand, were less adventurous and
relied more on their own memory rather than store cues to facilitate
choice. Invariably this choice was made from the chilled cabinet (not the
delicatessen counter) and was narrowly based, relying on product
familiarity for the final decision. With regard to specific product cues as
purchasing stimuli, we were surprised to find that product attributes such
as pack design, store marque or country of origin failed to prove
discriminatory.

In the concluding comments, suggestions for store adaptations to
encourage trial of these cheeses have been made. Since these adaptations
require modifications in staffing arrangements, merchandising at point-
of-purchase and product presentation, limited store tests are recom-
mended to determine the correct balance to optimise sales.

INTRODUCTION

During the 1980s, there has been a shift in the balance of power from
branded goods manufacturers to grocery retailers in the UK. This change
in market structure has had a significant effect on marketing at the product
level, and has led to a reduced investment behind manufacturers' brands
and continued growth of grocery retailers' own-label products (de
Chernatony and Knox 1991). Some researchers have questioned whether
consumers still perceive differences between these two tiers of grocery
branding (McGoldrick 1984). In some grocery markets, such as cheese,
retailer own-label products now dominate the market. As a consequence,
these retailers must be considered the market-makers and instrumental in
determining purchasing behaviour. We present evidence to suggest that,
within the continental sector[1] of the cheese market, the current strategy
adopted by multiple retailers as market-makers is less than optimal.
Survey research on the in-store behaviour of continental cheese
purchasers is reported. Their reliance on store cues and product cues at
point of purchase were found to vary with purchasing frequency. In the
light of these findings, a refocused product and merchandising strategy is
suggested and the managerial implications are considered.

CONTINENTAL CHEESES: MARKET GROWTH AND CHANGE AGENTS

Across mainland Europe, continuous growth of the cheese market has been sustained for the past decade, with increases of over 30 per cent in Germany, Italy and Holland (OECD 1979–88). Growth within these markets has been stimulated by an increased 'Europeanisation' of markets through cross-border movements of produce. The UK is no exception, although the comparable growth rate has been more modest at approximately 10 per cent. However, since the mid-1980s, continental cheese manufacturers have successfully penetrated the UK market and their sales have increased by 19 per cent (Milk Marketing Board 1989). Sales of continental cheeses[2] in the UK now stand at £98 million and the sector represents 12 per cent of the total cheese market (Dairy Crest 1988, 1989). Both the market penetration and consumption of continental cheeses continues to increase, against a general decline for traditional British cheeses such as Cheddar and Cheshire. For example, consumption of Dutch edam has increased by over 10 per cent in the five-year period to 1987, whilst English Cheddar has decreased by 2 per cent (MAFF 1985–9). Table 4.1 highlights a similar divergence in the household penetration of these cheeses and their counterparts.

Table 4.1   Types of cheese bought over a three-month period

Cheese type	1984 %	1987 %
Traditional UK Cheeses		
Cheddar	82	80
Cheshire	27	21
Leicester	20	21
Continentals		
Edam, Gouda	28	30
Blue veined	25	25
French	15	18

Source: BMRB 1987

As further deregulations occur in Europe, continental cheese manufacturers are likely to increase their marketing activities in the UK since it offers considerable development potential: UK cheese consumption per capita is currently half that of mainland Europe, at 8 kilos per annum. These manufacturers have been very quick to recognise the importance of the major multiple retailers, both as change agents in the marketing channel and in providing market access through direct delivery. The continued growth in sales of the continental cheeses is advantageous to multiple retailers because of the higher margins gained. The retailer's gross margin for continental cheese is 30–35 per cent, whilst for Cheddar cheese it is about 25 per cent. In common with other packaged goods markets (de Chernatony 1989), the major multiples now dominate the UK cheese market as a result of more concentrated buying power and the greater efficiency of larger stores (Office of Fair Trading 1985).

The next section considers the impact of retailer dominance in the continental cheese sector, and presents evidence of the growing need for a refocusing of marketing strategy.

THE FOCUS OF RETAILER STRATEGY

In 1987 the top five UK multiple retailers (Sainsbury, Tesco, Dee, Argyll and Asda) accounted for two-thirds of all continental cheese sales in the UK, and these sales represented about 11 per cent of their total cheese sales (AGB 1987). In the absence of sustained advertising by the manufacturers of continental cheeses (per cent of sterling sales; Retail Business 1985), the marketing of continentals is essentially a composite of separate retailer strategies. However, in each instance, their penetration strategy is rooted in a policy of stocking an extensive range of own-labels, and seems reliant on point-of-purchase impact to facilitate sales. Own-label products account for over half the continental cheese lines stocked (Liegl 1989). In common with other grocery markets, the multiples have seized the opportunity to innovate quality products under their own marque (King 1985). In effect, market growth of the sector has been driven by the introduction of own-label products, which now dominate the market sector in the absence of strongly branded competitors.

Increasingly, the traditional chilled-cabinet display area has also been supplemented by delicatessen counters that stock continental cheeses. The penetration of delicatessen counters in multiples is estimated to be between 75 and 90 per cent (Mintel 1988b).

It is our belief that under these rather unusual conditions where market penetration is being championed by own-label products, the major multiples need to refocus their strategy, since the provision of increased shelf-space alone may lead to diminishing returns. In fact, Liegl (1989) found that this situation may already have been reached. He concludes that the shelf-space now allocated to continental cheeses far outweighs the space merited on the basis of sales. For instance, he found that over 13 per cent of cheese shelf-space had been allocated to soft cheeses (mainly continentals), yet in sales terms these represent only 6 per cent of the cheese market in the multiple sector. This level of over-representation has also been observed by Thermistocli and Associates (1984) in a separate study.

Whilst it should be recognised that consumers are becoming more adventurous in their cheese-eating habits, and that continental cheese sales will also continue to grow as a result of increased snacking, the provision of an extensive product range may not in itself be a sufficient stimulus to alter short-term purchasing patterns. Since further market penetration of continental cheeses is likely to depend on the continued deployment of a 'push' strategy, retail marketers need to consider employing other facets of the retail marketing mix to increase consumption and frequency of purchase.

The purpose of our research was to carry out an exploratory market study amongst continental-cheese buyers to determine the level of interaction and influence which product and purchase situation (situational effects) have upon their purchasing decisions. Specifically, in the process of discriminating between the behaviours of occasional and frequent purchasers on salient product and situation factors, a refocused marketing strategy can be developed since any adaptation would be store based and, therefore, consistent with the current 'push' strategy.

SITUATIONAL DETERMINANTS IN CONSUMER BEHAVIOUR

There is a growing body of marketing literature which recognises the dualism of product and situation in consumer behaviour. From a behavioural standpoint, the two outside forces acting on the consumer are the product and the situation (the stimuli). The consumer reacts to the product and the situation, and decides on a product to be purchased (response). Equally, in a cognitive context, it is recognised that the interaction between the consumer, situation and product will result in a process of choice leading to behaviour (Assael 1987). Lewin (1933) discusses situational effects in their broadest context, which he describes as an 'environment'. In this sense, situations represent momentary encounters with those elements of the total environment which are available to the individual at a particular time. In a more confined unit of analysis, Barker (1968) developed the concept of a 'behavioural setting' which is an 'action pattern' bound in time and space.

The work of Keng and Ehrenberg (1984) on store loyalty can be viewed in this 'action pattern' context. They concluded that the low level of store loyalty displayed by consumers in purchasing grocery products was consistent across the retail chains studied, indicating that factors other than the appeal of the particular supermarket (store image, product range, location etc) intervened during the repeat purchase activity. In a study on the patronage of a new store, Kelly (1967) found that, although personal experiences of the store were of primary importance, word of mouth also had a determining influence. Ryans' work (1977) on electrical appliances concluded that store choice was dependent upon whether the product was purchased as a gift or for personal use. Similarly the impositions of time pressure (Mattson 1982) and the identifications of pre-purchase shopping problems (Claxton and Ritchie 1979) resulted in non-routine 'action patterns' of store choice.

In the context of within-store decision making, our particular framework, Belk (1975) argues that the intervening factors characterise a 'situation' and can be distinguished from both 'behavioural settings' and 'environment'. He offers five groups of situational characteristics which are consistent with the notion of 'situation':

1. *Physical surroundings.* Such factors as store decor, lighting and visible configurations of point-of-purchase displays surrounding the stimulus object.
2. *Social surroundings.* Other people accompanying the purchaser, and their interpersonal interactions in-store.
3. *Temporal perspective.* A dimension of situations which could affect the purchase decision, such as frequency of purchase, the time until the next/after the previous meal etc.
4. *Task definition.* An intention or requirement to obtain information about a specific purchase, also the possibility of differing buyer/user roles and consumption situations.
5. *Antecedent states.* Momentary moods (such as uncertainty, excitation) and momentary conditions (cash in hand, fatigue etc).

There is now considerable empirical evidence in support of Belk's taxonomy of 'situation'. Donovan and Rossiter (1982), in an environmental psychology approach, found that pleasure and arousal (engendered by store atmosphere) were significant mediators of intended shopping behaviours within the store. Gardner (1984), in a review of empirical studies on mood as a situational variable, highlights the importance of 'antecedent states' in purchasing decisions. Belk (1974), in a behavioural inventory study of in-store situations, established that anticipated consumption could explain much of the variance in meat and snack preferences.

The theory of scripted and non-scripted store behaviour, developed by Iyer (1989), is particularly germane to our study since it distinguished between planned and unplanned[3] purchasing events; the buying of continental cheeses is often considered to be unplanned (Mintel 1988a). Iyer restricts the meaning of 'script' to describe the purchase sequence. Hence, routine purchases which have an established purchasing sequence are scripted, whilst unplanned purchases represent a departure from script and memory. He found that routine purchases were invariably fulfilled, and unplanned purchases – where they occurred – took place only after routine purchases had been made. For these unplanned purchases, ie non-script behaviour, there was an increased reliance on external memory (store cues). In a more holistic study of planned and unplanned purchase behaviour, Cobb and Hoyer (1986) were able to categorise respondents into one of three purchaser groups – planners, partial planners and non-planners. Differences in cognitive styles were observed between groups. In distinguishing between their behaviour, it was found that for planners the product image and performance were key factors in the purchase decision. Partial and non-planners tended to postpone brand decisions until they reached the store.

It is clear from this brief review of literature that both product features and situational factors can directly influence purchasing behaviour. In recognition of the need to differentiate between the effects of situation and product (or object), and in attempting to operationalise a construct which has an existence apart from the individual's total consciousness, Belk (1975) offers a paradigm which is derivative of the more familiar stimulus-organism-response behavioural approach (Figure 4.1). In brief, the model attempts to separate the sources of influence on behaviour. This situation, it is suggested, can adequately be described by his taxonomy which we discussed earlier in this chapter. However, in limiting the construct in this way Belk also recognises the model's limitations: 'It is a false hope at this point to expect that we can systematically investigate a complete list of situational characteristics, because no such list exists'.

As a consequence, several studies have been critical of the value of Belk's model (Assael 1987, pp. 482–3). Others, though, have shown it to have validity (Belk 1979; Cavusgil and Cole 1981; Srivastava et al 1984).

From a retail strategy perspective Belk's model is very apposite, since it can evaluate both product and situational factors in the context of store purchase. Although the model has its limitations, we decided to use it to help evaluate behavioural differences between occasional and frequent

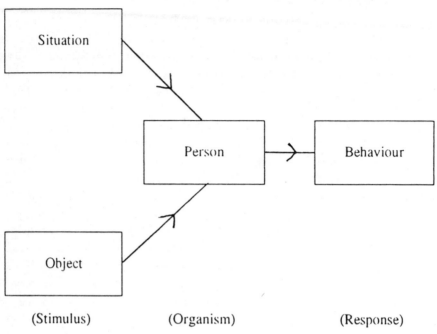

(Stimulus)   (Organism)   (Response)

Figure 4.1 Belk's revised S-O-R paradigm

purchasers of continental cheeses in reassessing the marketing mix at store level.

THE RESEARCH HYPOTHESES

Our research has been designed to distinguish between these two groups of purchasers across salient product and situational factors, in the belief that sales of continental cheeses can be enhanced if in-store effects can be understood, then modified to encourage more frequent purchases.

Our research hypotheses H2 and H3, which identify behavioural differences, have been derived both from the original work by Abelson (1976, 1981) on script behaviour and also its application to the in-store environment (Iyer 1989; Rethans and Taylor 1982). However, it was first necessary to test whether the model's predictor variables could correctly classify respondents according to their stated purchasing behaviour (H1), before component analysis could be applied with any degree of confidence. Thus, our research hypotheses can be summarised:

- H1: that the model's predictor variables could correctly classify consumers into one of the two membership groups that exhibit different purchasing behaviours, ie occasional and frequent purchasers of continental cheeses

74

- H2: frequent purchasers of continental cheeses follow a different script behaviour from occasional purchasers in-store, and are less reliant upon store cues in formulating a purchasing decision
- H3: frequent purchasers utilise differing product cues from occasional purchasers in facilitating choice at point of purchase.

METHODOLOGY

Individual depth interviews

Fifteen in-depth interviews were carried out amongst female respondents (both frequent and occasional purchasers) to explore in-store script behaviour and point-of-purchase decision variables.

Particular focus was given to the occasion of buying continental cheeses. Subsequently, modal variables were determined. In total, 23 predictor variables were identified and categorised as either 'situation' or 'object' stimuli according to Belk's classification procedures (1975). Nine of the 23 salient variables were situational and the remaining fourteen object stimuli (seven linked to product class and seven to product form respectively). These variables are listed in Table 4.2.

Main survey sample and questionnaire procedures

One hundred and fifty subjects for the main study were drawn from two areas of London, using a stratified, quota-sampling procedure. The sample frame was weighted in two directions to reflect purchasing habits (Mintel 1988a); 75 frequent purchasers of continental cheeses were recruited from the ABC1 member groups and 75 occasional purchasers from C2DE. All respondents were female and regularly used supermarkets for cheese purchases and each was interviewed using a personally administered questionnaire.

Respondents were screened on the basis of their purchasing frequency and categorised as frequent purchasers if they purchased continental cheese once a week or more, or occasional purchasers if once a month or less. Only these two respondent types were subsequently interviewed. Table 4.3 gives the classification results.

Since we were interested in comparative behaviours between groups (determined by 23 variables), the model was operationalised using discriminate analysis in order to test its efficacy in this context, and also to determine which of the variables contribute most in discriminating between behavioural patterns.

Table 4.2 Object and situation determinants

Situational determinants

(1)	TypeS	Number of different *types* of cheese bought per shopping occasion
(2)	Purfrea	*Frequency* of purchase of product class
(3)	Trial	Ask to *try* a certain cheese type
(4)	FamiliaO	*Familiarity* (of the purchases) with the product class
(5)	FamiliaS	*Familiarity* (of the purchaser) with the product form
(6)	Sure	*Uncertainty* in selection at P-o-P
(7)	Unplann	Likelihood of making an *unplanned* purchase
(8)	Advise	Ask *advice* from shop assistant on cheese types
(9)	Variety	Importance of having a *wide* variety at P-o-P

Object stimulus

	Product class		**Product form**
(10, 11)	TasteO	Like the *taste*	TasteS
(12, 13)	LabelO	Importance of *store (own) label*	LabelS
(14, 15)	VarietyO	Variety of *usage*	VarietyS
(16, 17)	DesignO	Packaging *design* appealing	DesignS
(18, 19)	PriceO	Lowest *price* around	PriceS
(20, 21)	KeepsO	*Keeps* a long time	KeepsS
(22, 23)	CountryO	Country of *origin*	CountryS

Notes: suffix O = product class   suffix S = product form
P-o-P = point of purchase

Table 4.3 Classification results

Actual group membership (no of respondents)[*]	Predicted group membership (no of respondents)	
	Occasional purchasers	**Regular purchasers**
Occasional purchasers (58)	86.2 per cent (50)	13.8 per cent (8)
Regular purchasers (75)	13.3 per cent (10)	86.7 per cent (65)
Regular classification rate: 86.5 per cent		

Note: [*] number of respondents = 133

Analysis technique

The raw data were processed with the SPSS statistical package using two-group Discriminate Analysis. Box's M-test was then carried out to ensure the equality of the two group covariance matrices. In this instance, a significance of 0.89 was obtained so the data set from 133 respondents[4] were deemed valid (Norusis 1988). In order to test the quality of the discriminate function, Wilks' Lambda was used. The small value of lambda obtained (0.49, p = .001) indicated that the function was good (Green and Tull 1988). The composition of the two membership groups is discussed in the next section as the efficacy of the modelling approach is explored (H1).

Wilks' Lambda was also calculated for each predictor variable of the discriminate function, and significances were determined so that H2 and H3 could be directly tested (see Table 4.4 in the next section).

RESULTS AND DISCUSSION

In order to determine the value of Belk's model in distinguishing behavioural differences, a classification test was carried out on the discriminate function. The classification matrix (Table 4.3) shows the predicted group membership against actual expressed behaviour. Overall, 87 per cent of respondents were correctly classified, indicating that the predictor variables discriminated very effectively between the two groups and that the criterion variable (purchase frequency) was appropriate.

The modelling approach H1 is shown to be valid.

To identify which of the predictor variables discriminated most effectively between the two groups, Wilks' Lambda was used as the criterion for selection; a probability level of less than 5 per cent was considered appropriate for this exploratory research. Table 4.4 shows the ordering of predictor variables according to their discriminatory power. Eight of the 23 variables significantly discriminated amongst the two groups of continental cheese purchasers; seven of the eight were situational factors and one was object stimulus. Thus, thirteen of the fourteen product-linked stimuli did not prove significantly discriminatory. On the basis of these rather clear results, a profile for both purchaser types can be developed to test H2 and H3.

Table 4.4 A classification of predictor variables based upon Belk's model

| | Stimulus type | | Wilk's Lambda | Significance |
	Situation	Object	λ	p
(1)	TypeS		0.81931	0.0000
(2)	Purfrea		0.85306	0.0000
(3)	Trial		0.91826	0.0009
(4)	FamiliaO		0.94871	0.0088
(5)	Sure		0.95497	0.0142
(6)		PriceS	0.95766	0.0175
(7)	Unplann		0.95804	0.0180
(8)	Advice		0.96487	0.0307
(9)		TasteS	0.97846	0.0918
(10)		LabelS	0.99525	0.4305
(11)		VarietyO	0.99643	0.4943
(12)	Variety		0.99656	0.5025
(13)		LabelO	0.99762	0.5768
(14)		VarietyS	0.99814	0.6223
(15)		DesignS	0.99825	0.6325
(16)		PriceO	0.99853	0.6611
(17)		KeepsO	0.99913	0.7359
(18)		TasteO	0.99915	0.7387
(19)	FamiliaS		0.99953	0.8051
(20)		KeepsS	0.99989	0.9058
(21)		CountryO	0.99992	0.9173
(22)		CountryS	0.9999	0.9735
(23)		DesignO	1.0000	0.9844

Notes: suffix O = product class
suffix S = product form

Frequent purchasers of continental cheeses

Not unexpectedly, frequent purchasers of continental cheeses tend to buy more types of cheese (TypeS) and purchase from within the product class more frequently (Purfrea). Their script behaviour within the store was also significantly different from that of occasional purchasers. However, the picture which emerges is contrary to our expectations and research hypothesis (H2); frequent purchasers are more reliant on store cues in formulating a purchasing decision than are occasional purchasers. For instance, at the provision counter they will frequently seek shop assistants' advice on cheese types (Advice) and ask to taste a sample (Trial). As a consequence, at point of purchase their selection of continental cheeses is more assured (Sure) than occasional purchasers. Equally, as a result of their behavioural pattern in-store, frequent purchasers are more prepared to make unplanned purchases of continental cheeses (Unplann).

H2 is rejected.

Occasional purchasers of continental cheeses

The occasional purchaser is less adventurous in her script behaviour, relying more on internal memory than external store cues in facilitating choice. Invariably this choice is made from the chilled cabinet and is tempered by a feeling of uncertainty; hence the need to rely upon familiarity (FamiliaO).

With regard to specific product cues or stimuli, we were surprised to find that, with the exception of price (PriceS), none of the remaining 13 product variables proved discriminatory. In a sense this finding must be seen by retailer marketers as disturbing, since neither group appears to favour a specific array of product cues at point of purchase. In particular, neither country of origin (CountryS), nor the own-label marque (LabelS) or pack design (DesignS) were identified by either group.

In a market sector dominated by own-label products primarily sourced from countries in mainland Europe, one would expect to find a level of selectivity and discrimination based upon brand name cues (Cox 1967). Our exploratory research has shown this not to be the case.

H3 is rejected.

Intuitively, one might also expect frequent purchasers of continental cheeses to have developed stronger instrumental values for certain products based upon such factors as taste (TasteS) and usage situations (VarietyS). The fact that our empirical evidence does not support this notion suggests a lack of attitudinal-behavioural consistency towards the attitude object (Foxall 1983, 1984). However, in the broader context of store purchasing behaviour in which situational factors as well as product stimuli are considered, consistencies in attitude and behaviour did emerge for both purchaser types as the discriminant analysis has shown. However, in common with Iyer's research findings (1989), our research has also shown that situational effects within the store can sometimes modify purchase behaviour. This was found to be particularly true of frequent purchasers, since their script behaviour involves a greater exposure to in-store cues which may lead to unplanned purchases of the product. On the other hand, occasional purchasers of continental cheeses did not exhibit such a marked search behaviour and were, consequently, more cautious in their purchasing behaviour, using price (PriceS) and a limited choice set as a mechanism for risk reduction. Current store practices seem ineffectual in stimulating choice or more frequent purchases amongst this group.

Retailers now need to reassess how both situational factors and product cues can be used to increase sales of continental cheeses. Adaptations in product, merchandising and staffing arrangements are outlined in the next section.

Store adaptations

In order to sustain growth in this market sector, retail management needs to encourage trial of its own-label products, particularly amongst occasional purchasers. This could be achieved in a number of ways. By marginally relocating items, shoppers are likely to increase their reliance on external cues since their knowledge of the store environment would be depleted. In order to draw both types of purchaser to the delicatessen counter, merchandising material at the chilled cabinet could encourage use of a cheese advisory and trial tasting service based at that counter. Country of origin leaflets describing the various cheese types could also be made available at point of purchase. In addition, both snack and recipe suggestions could be combined in a give-away educational booklet.

With regard to product cues, the packaging would appear to be a key component that could easily be modified cost-effectively, given the dominance of own-label products. Possibly, by using different colours to distinguish country of origin and by introducing bolder branding to separate cheese types, selection procedures may be simplified, particularly for occasional purchasers.

CONCLUSIONS

The present research was undertaken to determine the level of interaction and influence which product and situational determinants have on the purchasing decision of continental cheese consumers. Belk's revised S-O-R model was seen as being particularly germane, and was selected for our exploratory work. In distinguishing between frequent and occasional purchasers of continental cheeses, it has been possible to develop a discriminant function with very good classification power in validating our modelling approach. The script behaviour for frequent purchasers of continental cheeses was found to be significantly different from that of the occasional purchaser. Both have been deduced from the significant variables in the discriminant function, and are considered to be the key to inducing behavioural change. Rather surprisingly, product cues were not found to be discriminatory, casting further doubt on the belief in attitudinal-behavioural consistencies for low involvement products of this type.

It is argued that, if further growth is to be sustained in a market sector dominated by own labels, the retail marketing mix must be refocused. The researchers have suggested adaptations in product, merchandising and staffing arrangements that are consistent with the maintenance of a 'push' strategy in this market sector. However, determining the correct balance in the adaptations suggested is an empirical question that can best be measured in limited store tests.

Notes

1. Cheese products manufactured in mainland Europe.
2. Does not include the category 'continental processed' eg Kraft or Kavli which are now both manufactured in mainland Europe.
3. Authors use the word 'impulse' synonymously with 'unplanned'; the latter is used throughout the chapter.
4. Seventeen of the 150 returns were excluded since at least one question had not been fully answered.

REFERENCES

Ableson R P (1976), 'Script processing in attitude formation and decision making', Carroll J S and Payne J W (eds), in *Cognition and Social Behaviour*, Erlbaum, Hillsdale, N J.

—(1981), 'Psychological status of the script concept', *American Psychologist*, 36, pp 715–29.

AGB Attwood Statistics (1987), made available from the Milk Marketing Board, Surrey.

Assael H (1987), *Consumer Behaviour and Marketing Action*, Kent Publishing Company, Boston, Mass.

Barker R G (1968), *Ecological Psychology: Concepts and Methods for studying the Environment of Human Behaviour*, Stanford University Press, California.

Belk R W (1974), 'An Exploratory Assessment of Situational Effects in Buyer Behaviour', *Journal of Marketing Research*, 11 (May), pp 156–63.

—(1975), 'Situational Variables and Consumer Behaviour', *Journal of Consumer Research*, 2 (Dec), pp 157–63.

—(1979), 'A Free Response Approach to Developing Product-Specific Consumption Situation Taxonomies', in Shocker A D (ed), *Analytic Approaches to Product and Market Planning*, Marketing Science Institute, Cambridge, Mass.

Cavusgil S T and Cole C A (1981), 'An Empirical Investigation of Situational, Attitudinal and Personal Influences on Behavioural Intentions', in Bernard K (ed), *Proceedings of the American Marketing Association Educators' Conference*, 47, pp 210–25.

Claxton J D and Ritchie J R B (1979), 'Consumer Prepurchase Shopping Problems: A Focus on the Retailing Component', *Journal of Retailing*, 55 (fall), pp 24–46.

Cobb C J and Hoyer W D (1986), 'Planned versus Impulse Purchase Behaviour', *Journal of Retailing*, 62 (winter), pp 384–409.

Cox D F (1967), 'The Sorting rule Model of the Consumer Product Evaluation Process', in Cox D F (ed), *Risk Taking and Information Handling in Consumer Behaviour*, Harvard University Press, Boston, Mass.

Dairy Crest (1988), *Annual Report and Accounts*, Surrey.

—(1989), *Dairy Cabinet Report*, Surrey.

de Chernatony L (1989), 'Understanding Consumer's Perceptions of Competitive Tiers – Can Perceived Risk Help?', *Journal of Marketing Management*, 4 (3), pp 288–99.

de Chernatony L and Knox S, 'Consumers' Ability to Correctly Recall Grocery Prices', paper at the XXIII UK Marketing Educators' Conference, July, Cardiff University.

Donovan R J and Rossiter J R (1982), 'Store Atmosphere: An Environmental Psychology Approach', *Journal of Retailing*, 58 (spring), pp 34–57.

Foxall G (1983), 'Evidence for Attitudinal Behavioural Consistency: Implications for Consumer Research Paradigms', *Marketing and Logistics Discussion Paper Series*, Cranfield Institute of Technology, Bedford.

—(1984), 'Consumer Behaviour in Food Markets: Problems of Predicting Choice in New Product Development', paper at the Agricultural Economics Society Conference, 30 June, Sheffield Polytechnic.

Gardner M P (1984), 'The Consumer's Mood: An Important Situational Variable', in Kinnear T (ed), *Advances in Consumer Research*, XI, pp 525–9, Association for Consumer Research, Ann Arbor, Mich.

Green P and Tull D (1988), *Research for Marketing Decisions*, fifth edition, Prentice-Hall, Englewood Cliffs, NJ.

Iyer E S (1989), 'Unplanned Purchasing: Knowledge of Shopping Environment and Time Pressure', *Journal of Retailing*, 65 (spring), pp 40–57.

Kelly R F (1967), 'The Role of Information in the Patronage Decision: A Diffusion Phenomenon', in Moyer M S and Vosburgh R E (eds), *Marketing for Tomorrow ... Today*, American Marketing Association, Chicago.

Keng K A and Ehrenberg A S C (1984), 'Patterns of Store Choice', *Journal of Marketing Research*, 11, pp 399–409.

King S (1985), 'Another turning point for brands?', *Admap*, 519 (Oct), pp 480–4.

Lewin K (1933), 'Environmental Forces in Child Behaviour and Development', in Murchison C C (ed), *A Handbook of Child Psychology*, second edition, revised, Clark University Press, Worcester, Mass.

Liegl J (1989) 'Marketing Opportunities for German Cheese in the United Kingdom', MSc thesis, Silsoe College, Cranfield Institute of Technology, Bedford.

MAFF (1985–9), *Household Food Consumption and Expenditure*, Annual Report of the National Food Survey Committee, Ministry of Agriculture, Fisheries and Food, London.

Mattson B E (1982), 'Situational Influences on Store Choice', *Journal of Retailing*, 58 (fall), pp 46–58.

McGoldrick P (1984), 'Grocery Generics – An Extension of the Private Label Concept', *European Journal of Marketing*, 18 (1), pp 5–24.

Milk Marketing Board (1989), *EEC Dairy Facts and Figures*, Surrey.

Mintel Intelligence (1988a), *Cheese*, Mintel Publications Limited, London.

—(1988b), *Delicatessen Foods*, Mintel Publications Limited, London.

Norusis M J (1988), *SPSS/PC+ Advanced Statistics TM V2.0*, SPSS Inc, Chicago, Illinois.

OECD (1979–88), *Food Consumption Statistics 1979–88*, Organisation for Economic Co-operation and Development, Paris.

Office of Fair Trading (1985), *Competition and Retailing*, HMSO, London.

Retail Business (1985), *Cheese Special Report no 2*, ref 331, Economist Publications Limited, London.

Rethans A J and Taylor J L (1982), 'A Script Theoretic Analysis of Consumer Decision Making', in Michell A (ed), *Advances in Consumer Research*, IX, Association for Consumer Research, Ann Arbor, Mich.

Ryans A B (1977), 'Consumer Gift Buying Behaviour: An Exploratory Analysis', in Greenber B A and Bellengereds D W (eds), *Proceedings of the American Marketing Association Educators' Conference*, 41, pp 99–104.

Srivastava R K, Alpert M I and Shocker A D (1984), 'A Consumer-Orientated Approach for Determining Market Structures', *Journal of Marketing*, 48, pp 32–45.

Thermistocli and Associates (1984), *The Secret of the Own Brand*, London.

5

ATTITUDE, PERSONAL NORMS AND INTENTIONS*

Simon Knox and Leslie de Chernatony

OUTLINE

During 1983 there was a national water strike in the UK. As a result, sales of bottled mineral water leaped by over 50 per cent within a year and, each year since then, volume growth has been sustained at well over 10 per cent. In the last few years, sales of these brands through supermarkets have begun to significantly outweigh the traditional market channels of pubs, restaurants, bistros etc, and a plethora of own-label brands have become well entrenched in the market. All the evidence suggests that a mass-market has evolved from the niche-market established by Perrier in London during the 1980s. According to the CEO of Leo Burnett Advertising, the Perrier Agency, the brand was originally positioned to appeal to image-conscious trendies and the advertising created to reflect style, fashion and success. Mineral water was established as an expressive product; one which lent itself to demonstrations of status amongst the cognoscenti.

Given the way that the market has evolved and radically altered with new competition and distributive channels, we wanted to find out if consumers still saw the brands in this way. So, our primary research task was to determine the saliency of both normative and behavioural beliefs amongst users of bottled mineral water. We argued, a priori, that product-derived benefits would now significantly outweigh the influence of social conspicuousness as the main reason for consumption.

In this chapter, we present an argument in favour of using the Extended Fishbein Model (EFM) to measure beliefs both about drinking the product and the social consequences. Once the model was validated using the aggregate database, the data were disaggregated into four respondent cells characterised by consumption criteria. By applying principal

---

* This chapter first appeared in Moutinho L, Brownlie D and Livingstone J (eds) (1989), *Marketing Audit of the 80s* Vol 1.

components analysis, we then looked at the degree to which these product-performance beliefs and social norms variously influenced each of these groups. We were able to detect differences in the balance of behavioural influences for heavy, medium and light users. We also contrasted these findings with the fourth group, non-users of the product category.

Finally, using median tests we searched for attitude-behaviour consistency across groups. By measuring evaluations of product-performance beliefs, we were able to demonstrate an extraordinary degree of correspondence which would seem to signpost that behavioural characteristics directly determine the saliency of attitudes towards consumption. Further managerial conclusions are drawn out from the research findings, accepting the limitations of small-sample research and the validity of multiple regression analysis.

EUROPEAN CONSUMPTION OF MINERAL WATER

Since the Second World War, mineral water markets have been successfully created in Western Europe and the USA. France leads the world in consumption of mineral waters, at 72 litres per capita (Table 5.1), and remains the leading producer.

Table 5.1 Per Capita Consumption of Mineral Water (litres)

Country	Litres
France	72
Belgium	54
Italy	54
Spain	20
USA	20
Holland	9
UK	2

Some 70 per cent of French people regularly drink the product. However, since the early 1980s, French domestic sales of both the sparkling and still water have remained static. During this time, exports of both products from France have grown dramatically, spearheaded by the efforts of the market leader, the Source Perrier Company, which had a product portfolio of some fifteen brands including Perrier, Volvic and Buxton. In the USA, Perrier accounts for about 86 per cent of all imported water and is market leader with a 30 per cent share (Betts 1988). Source Perrier has also been instrumental in developing the UK market. Since 1972, when

Perrier (UK) was formed, the UK market has been dominated by Source Perrier brands.

MINERAL WATERS IN THE UK

During the 1970s, Perrier built the market almost single handed, aided by the 'Eau so successful' advertising campaign devised by Leo Burnett. By the early 1980s, there were five major competitors each contributing to advertising spend and stimulating market growth (Table 5.2).

In 1983, there was a major marketing windfall, a national water strike, which caused the market to leap by almost 50 per cent in one year. At the same time, the market began to segment on a price basis, as the premium brands gained national distribution through grocery outlets and own labels were introduced.

Table 5.2: The UK mineral water market (million litres)

Year	Litres
1980	25
1982	34
1984	65
1986	105
1987	150
1990	210

Source: Perrier UK estimates

Today, the ownership of the leading mineral water brands can be divided between those companies that have a diversified product range, such as Nestlé, Cadbury Schweppes and BSN, and those which are purely mineral water producers (eg Source Perrier, Highland Spring).

Whilst product lifecycle theory suggests that volume growth will inevitably slow down, Perrier estimate that the average Briton will be drinking 10 litres of bottled water a year by the end of the century (Thompson 1986). Their survey research showed that 34 per cent of UK adults claimed to drink bottled mineral water, 25 per cent once a month or more.

THE UK CONSUMER AND DERIVED BRAND BENEFITS

Forty-one per cent of UK mineral water is consumed by Londoners. This may be due to the fact that the original 'eau' campaign was targeted at 'image-conscious trendies' who saw mineral water as a status symbol (Source Perrier 1987). Perrier was associated with style, fashion and success. The press and poster campaign was London- and Southern-based to complement the distribution channels which were primarily through the on-trade: hotels, bistros, restaurants and pubs. Thus, the intention was to establish mineral water as an expressive product; one which lends itself to demonstrations of status.

As the distribution base broadens (56 per cent of national sales are distributed through major multiples; Mintel 1988), a mass-market has developed from the niche position previously occupied.

There is also considerable evidence to suggest that other environmental and social factors are contributing to structural change. Thompson (1986) writes '... there has been an increased awareness of the fact that tap drinking water has been subjected to multiple recycling; concern about chemical additives (to tap water) such as fluoride; worries about the effects of industrial and farming pollution, especially nitrates, and changes in drinking habits with younger people looking for alternatives to spirits'. Richard Foulsham, managing director of BSN, has suggested that the drink-drive factor has made an important contribution to increased sales of mineral water. He concludes that this is due to a psychological shift in consumers' perceptions, with soft drinks increasingly seen as acceptable alternatives to alcohol (*Marketing Week* 1986).

If one accepts the premise that bottled mineral water has now evolved from niche branding to mass-market, one also needs to recognise that consumers' attitude towards the brands and their perceived benefits are likely to have shifted with increasing product availability. Under these market penetration conditions, the brands are likely to be perceived with less status value and more instrumentally, ie benefits derived from personal satisfactions. Clearly, this typology is unlikely to be mutually exclusive since many brands offer both expressive and instrumental values. On balance, it is our contention that there has been a shift in consumer buying behaviour, attitude and intention which places the product category firmly towards the utilitarian end of this continuum.

The purpose of our research was to carry out an exploratory market study to test this hypothesis by constructing and validating a multi-attribute model of the product category in the UK. If the disaggregated data did prove to be sufficiently discriminatory, the model could also be used as a basis for segmentation and to trace attitude-behaviour correspondence.

THE ROLE OF ATTITUDES IN INFLUENCING CONSUMER BEHAVIOUR

Traditional marketing research appears to be based on the assumption that an understanding of consumers' attitudes will provide some guidance as to likely behaviour, even though a knowledge of attitudes will not guarantee a reliable forecast of a specific type of behaviour. Whilst there has been a considerable amount of research into this relationship (eg Day and Deutscher 1982), the fact that 'attitude' has been defined in over 100 different ways with at least as many different measurement approaches (Fishbein 1967) undermines any categorical understanding of the attitude-behaviour relationship. The most widely accepted definition of attitude is that from Allport: 'learned predispositions to respond to an object or class of objects in a consistently favourable or unfavourable way'.

The framework generally held for understanding attitudes is based upon three components: cognitive (beliefs about the particular object), affective (feelings or evaluation regarding the attitude object) and conative (behavioural tendencies towards the object); The relationship between differing patterns of these three components is thought to characterise the nature of attitude (Krech and Crutchfield 1962). Consideration of market research procedures shows that attitude measurement techniques tend often to be unidimensional scalings of either beliefs about brands or evaluations of brands (Sampson and Harris 1970). Also, these measures often focus upon consumers' attitudes towards brands, rather than their attitudes towards buying the brand (cf Levitt's classic observation in 1970 that industrial purchasers buy quarter-inch holes, not quarter-inch drills).

In developing the Theory of Reasoned Action, a new era of attitude research was introduced by Fishbein and Ajzen (1975, 1980), who stressed the difference between attitude and belief (i.e. the probability of the object having a specific relationship with some other object or value). They viewed attitude as an unidimensional concept based upon the amount of affect for an object, and defined attitude as a 'learned implicit response that mediates evaluative behaviour'. They also argued that researchers need to study four variables to understand consumer behaviour better: actual behaviour, behavioural intentions, attitudes and beliefs. In the model (the Extended Fishbein Model) they postulate that overall behaviour can be inferred from behavioural intention, which is a function of:

1. The individual's attitude toward performing the behaviour in a given situation,
2. the norms governing that behaviour in that situation and the person's motivation to comply with these norms.

So, the model takes the form:

$$B \approx BI = W1 \text{ [Attitude to act]} + W2 \text{ [influencing norms]} + E \tag{1}$$

$$\text{Attitude to act (Aact)} = \Sigma_i \, b_i e_i \tag{2}$$

$$\text{Influencing norm (SN)} = \Sigma i \, (nbj) \, (mcj) \tag{3}$$

where:

B	=	actual behaviour
BI	=	behavioural intention
b_i	=	salient belief about an outcome of the behaviour
e_i	=	evaluative aspect of the possible outcome (ie relative desirability of each outcome)
nb_j	=	normative belief, ie respondents' belief about what salient referents would advise
mc_j	=	motivation to comply with the wishes of the referent
$W1, W2$ =		weighting factors (beta weights)
E	=	residual term.

From a marketing perspective, this model is very apposite since it evaluates a consumer's attitudes toward consuming or purchasing a product rather than the attitude toward the product itself. Whilst someone may have a very positive attitude towards a Porsche, there may be a negative attitude to purchasing because of the price. Also, by including the effects from referent groups, the model can offer a broader account of other behavioural influences.

The virtue of this model is that it tries to simplify the complex process of consumer behaviour. However, it is not without its weaknesses. The first is the assumed relationship between behavioural intention and actual behaviour. As the time between measurement of intentions and actual behaviour increases, factors can intervene to change the original intention. Factors which can weaken the assumed relationship include unforeseen situational and environmental events as well as the response to new information. Secondly, if consumers feel a low level of involvement with the product category, they are likely to only have a few weakly held beliefs in memory upon which to base attitudes and behavioural intentions. There is then the danger that intentions remain transitory and may vary as time elapses. Thirdly, there is the problem that both the attitudinal and the normative beliefs may relate to the same influencing source which would complicate any attempt to identify whether Aact or SN primarily determines the behavioural response. As a consequence, several studies have been critical of the value of the Extended Fishbein Model (see Wilkie 1986 for details). Others though have shown the model to have predictive validity in both the laboratory (Bonfield 1974; Wilson et al 1975) and the marketplace (Ryan and Bonfield 1980; Tuck 1973).

Recognising the limitations of the Extended Fishbein Model, we decided to use it, as we believed it could provide guidance on understanding consumer behaviour in this particular market.

THE RESEARCH HYPOTHESES

Since the purpose of the research was to provide a measure of consumer behaviour, attitudes and social influences relevant to the mineral water market, the Extended Fishbein Model (EFM) was selected as being the most appropriate device for the purpose. However, it was first necessary to establish the predictive validity of the model before component analysis could be applied with any degree of confidence. Thus, our research hypotheses can be summarised:

- H1: that the EFM is a valid predictor of consumption behaviour in the mineral water market, accounting for more than 60 per cent of the variance in behavioural intentions.
- H2: that the perceived benefits derived from consumption stem from personal satisfactions rather than from the effects of social conspicuousness.

METHODOLOGY

Individual depth interviews

In order to elicit behavioural and normative beliefs regarding the drinking of bottled water, 25 in-depth interviews were carried out amongst respondents using a free response format. Eighty per cent of the sample were female and 25 years old or more; 60 per cent were in the $C_1 C_2$ socio-economic category. Twenty per cent of interviewees were drawn from non-users aware of the product category. Modal attitudinal and normative beliefs were identified as outlined by Fishbein and Ajzen (1980); in total, there were twelve salient attitudinal beliefs and seven salient referents derived by data reduction of the 25 taped interviews. These belief statements are listed in Table 5.3.

Table 5.3: Attitudinal beliefs and salient referents

Attitudinal beliefs

Drinking bottled water:
1. Provides a source of water free from impurities
2. Provides a drink free from additives
3. Provides a drink which is alcohol free
4. Provides a refreshing drink
5. Gives me a drink with no calories
6. Provides a drink which is healthy
7. Provides a non-alcoholic drink when driving
8. Will help me control my weight
9. Offers an alternative taste to soft drinks
10. Tastes the same as drinking tap water
11. Provides a mixer with other drinks
12. Is a waste of money

Normative beliefs

Referent influences include:
13. The family
14. The doctor
15. Close friends
16. Articles in the press
17. Advertisements on TV
18. Media personalities
19. Fellow members of sporting and social groups

Main survey sample

One hundred subjects for the main study were drawn from the Anglian TV region at three sampling points. The region was selected for two principal reasons:

1. According to the *Which?* report on tap water, the region does not meet EEC standards for principal drinking water pollutants.
2. The region now has a higher overall level of bottled water consumption per capita than London or Southern TV areas (Mintel 1988).

In this area of the country, the sample population would be most likely to hold beliefs about the consumption of bottled water which reflected both utilitarian and socially derived benefits.

A stratified, quota sampling technique was used to ensure that four user groups (heavy, medium, light and non-users) were included. In the event, the researchers were able to recruit 25 respondents into each of these four cells. The sample was weighted towards women ABs in the 25–44 age group, identified by Mintel Market Intelligence (1988) as being the highest-consuming categories. No attempt was made to differentiate between individual brands or water types (still or carbonated).

Measuring behaviour and behavioural intentions (BI)

The dependent variable

Behavioural intention was measured amongst users and non-users by asking how often respondents intended to drink bottled water in the next month. Each respondent was then placed into one of ten consumption categories based upon the Mintel classification. These ten behavioural categories were then used as a basis for constructing a behavioural intention index, corresponding to the BI component in equation 1. As a cross-reference, respondents were also asked how often they drank bottled water at present (B in equation 1) and there was very little difference between stated current behaviour and intentions over the next month. (It would have been more rigorous methodologically to measure behaviour by collecting labels or empty bottles after a one-month period but time did not permit in this exploratory study.) The questionnaire was administered over a two-week period during the summer of 1988 so that any seasonal influences on consumption would not vary significantly.

Analysis

The raw data were analysed in two phases. Firstly, regression analysis was carried out and regression correlations (R) and their corrected values $(R)^2$ were computed using Minitab. In addition, summed scores for Aact (equation 2) and SN (equation 3) could also be calculated using this software.

Secondly, disaggregate analysis was carried out on the attitudinal data using SPSS so that the characteristics of discrete user groups could be identified and attitude-behaviour correspondence between groups examined.

RESULTS AND DISCUSSION

A major objective of the study was to determine the extent to which the EFM could predict behavioural intention. Table 5.4 shows the beta weights and multiple regression coefficients obtained for the model specified in equation 1 and, also, for two additional models incorporating the attitudinal and normative components separately. In the full model, attitudinal and normative components together accounted for 75 per cent of the variation in behavioural intention. In the other two models tested, attitude alone accounted for 72 per cent of the variation in behavioural intention, whilst subjective norm alone accounted for 47 per cent of the variation.

Table 5.4 Regression analysis results

Regression models	Average regression Beta Wt W1	Average regression Beta Wt W2	Average multiple R	Corrected average R^2
$BI = W1A_{act} + W2SN + E$	0.72**	0.17	0.87**	0.75
$BI = W1A_{act} + E$	0.85**	–	0.85**	0.72
$BI = W2SN + E$	–	0.69**	0.69**	0.47

Note: ** = $p < 0.05$

With regard to the intention to consume mineral water, the EFM was thus shown to have good predictive power (accepting the validity of the assumptions underlying the use of multiple regression models):

H1 is shown to be valid.

The relative magnitudes of the beta weights W1 (0.72) and W2 (0.17) in the full regression model in Table 5.4 suggest that attitudes influence behavioural intentions about drinking bottled water more strongly than normative influences. This is borne out by the correlations of the two independent variables (Aact and SN) with BI (see second and third models in Table 5.4). R^2 values of 0.72 and 0.47 were obtained for these component contributions when assessed individually. In consumer behaviour research, it seems reasonable to assume that differences in predictive usefulness (as measured by beta weights) for normative versus attitude beliefs will reflect the degree of social conspicuousness versus the need for personal satisfaction with product performance (Bourne 1964; Cohen and Barbar 1970). In this instance, the attitudinal component significantly outranked the normative component from which one can infer that these brands are now drunk primarily for 'instrumental' rather than 'expressive' reasons. Whilst the researchers have no empirical evidence to suggest that the reverse was true during the early 1980s, the historical development of the advertising and distribution strategy suggests that this was the underlying assumption of the manufacturers.

H2 is shown to be valid.

Differentiating between user groups

To assess whether the different groups of respondents (ie non-users, light, medium and heavy users) considered the same basic dimensions to formulate their behavioural intentions, a principal components analysis of their beliefs and social norms that influence their mineral water consumption was undertaken. This technique is a powerful data reduction device which has also been used in several research projects to determine the key attributes of different consumer groups (see Churchill 1983 for details). For each of the four respondent groups separately, attention was focused on the matrices of the 25 cases × 19 variables (ie the 12 elements of the beliefs about drinking mineral water and the 7 social norms). Correlations between these 19 variables were calculated and, using the SPSS suite of programs, the 4 correlation matrices were subjected to principal components analysis.

Examination of the non-rotated component loadings did not provide a particularly illuminating picture so a Varimax rotation was applied to those components with eigenvalues greater than 1 (between 6 and 9 components depending on the respondent group). For each of the 4 respondent groups, it was found that the first 5 components explained approximately 60 per cent of the variance. To interpret the meaning of these components, only those variables that had the highest loadings on each of the rotated components were considered. Table 5.5 summarises these high loading variables for each of the 4 groups.

A visual inspection of the variables shows that there are similarities across the three user groups (eg the alcohol-free, additive-free nature of the brands) which clearly distinguish users from non-users since members of the latter group do not recognise these benefits. Indeed, they appear to hold only weak or negative beliefs about drinking mineral water brands in general. What is really interesting, though, is that in comparison to the heavy user of mineral water, the non-user is strongly influenced by social norms, whilst the heavy user has a wide repertoire of product-derived beliefs and shows much less reliance upon social norm influences. For instance, the behavioural intentions of non-users are strongly influenced by the press, close friends, media personalities and TV ads whilst product-derived beliefs are very limited. By contrast, heavy users hold broad-ranging beliefs about these brands, which include that they represent value for money, and are healthy and impurity and alcohol free. Their normative influences appear more removed, and are limited to social groups, the press and media personalities.

Table 5.5   Sources of influences across user groups

Component	Mineral water user status			
	⸜ **Non-users**	**Light**	**Medium**	**Heavy**
1	Influenced by press	Refreshing and alcohol-free Influenced by press	Additive and alcohol free	Influenced by social groups Value for money Impurity free
2	Influenced by friends and media personalities	Influenced by TV advert and doctor	A healthy drink and an alternative to soft drinks Influenced by social group	Alcohol free Influenced by press
3	Helps control weight	Influenced by media personalities. Additive free	Influenced by family Refreshing and helps control weight	Influenced by media personalities Healthy drink
4	Influenced by TV advertisements	Tap water taste	Influenced by TV advertisements	Tap water taste
5	Waste of money but is an alternative to soft drinks	An alternative to soft drinks and helps control weight	Influenced by media personalities and close friends	Alternative soft drink

Finally, Median tests were carried out for each of the 19 variables so that average scores amongst each for the four user groups could be determined and consistencies (or differences) between groups investigated. What was particularly striking about these median scores was the level of attitude/behaviour correspondence they showed. For example, eight of the ten salient belief statements about consumption showed significant differences in the scores for each group ($p = 0.05$); a heavy-to-non-user order was maintained. This result further validates the view that attitudes (and beliefs) about consuming low-involvement brands of this type are strengthened by usage.

Managerial implications

Recognising the limitations of small sample research, the results tentatively indicate that the non-user and the heavy user of mineral water may be differentiated, with the former being more concerned about their perceptions of influencing social norms rather than their constellation of beliefs. These results would benefit from further testing amongst a larger sample and, if replicated, they could help develop marketing strategies. For example, by using qualitative research amongst non-users, the influence of social norms could be explored and the marketing offering suitable altered (eg PR and sales promotions strategies). Likewise, research could be undertaken amongst heavy users to assess whether their beliefs about individual brands of mineral waters reflected the manufacturer's selling proposition, and a revised communications strategy suitably developed.

CONCLUSIONS

The present research was undertaken to test the efficiency of multi-attribute modelling in predicting consumer behaviour in the UK mineral water market. It was argued that the Extended Fishbein Model would be appropriate for this exploratory research based upon the marketing literature. The research has shown that the model has good predictive power under the conditions in which behavioural intentions and behaviour were judged by the respondents. With the model measuring both attitudes towards a given behaviour and the social influences, it has been possible to discount the notion that the current market growth is based upon the 'designer water' concept since the evidence suggests that instrumental or utilitarian values are now more important than status-derived benefits.

Principal components analysis found that non-users were more concerned about influential norms, while heavy users had a constellation of beliefs about mineral waters. For the heavier user, consumption appears based upon a risk-reduction process (drinking mineral water due to concerns about tap water pollution). Non-users do not seem to value the benefits of mineral water and, while apparently aware of media activity, are insufficiently disposed to modify their behaviour.

These disaggregated data also provided convincing evidence to suggest that attitudinal-behavioural consistency varied according to frequency of usage, which lends further weight to the behaviouristic approach. That is, for low involvement products of this type, behavioural change is necessary before the formation of stable attitudes (see Krugman 1965, 1967; Foxall 1990).

Whilst the researchers recognised that it was never the intention to measure individual brand benefits (or derived benefits to be more precise), the salient beliefs do appear to be highly generic to the market.

The growth in own-label products and their use of supplier brand names bears witness to this generic market idea. However, the forecasts seem to be suggesting that market growth will continue in the short term and that household penetration should also increase as uncertainty about tap water purity continues to be reported in the media. Source Perrier, as the market maker and leader, continues to provide an awareness function through its media advertising. Spadel, on the other hand, has recognised the importance of associating its Spa brand with body purity and health; last year, the company ran a black and white campaign in the quality press with this positioning. It remains to be seen how effective Perrier remains in arresting the advances of brands that successfully communicate product-derived benefits now that the niche-market has evolved into a mass-market and 'designer water' is a thing of the past.

REFERENCES

Betts P (1988), *Financial Times*, 13 January.

Bonfield E H (1974), 'Attitude, social influence, personal norms and Intention Interactions as related to brand purchase behaviour', *Journal of Marketing Research*, 11, pp 379–89.

Bourne F S (1964), 'Group Influence in Marketing', in Day R L (ed), *Marketing Models: Quantitative and Behavioural*, Scranton Pa International, London.

Churchill G (1983), *Marketing Research*, Dryden Press, Chicago.

Day G S and Deutscher T (1982), 'Attitudinal predictions of choice of major appliance brands', *Journal of Marketing Research*, 19 (May), pp 192–8.

Cohen J B and Barbar A M (1970), 'An interactive consumer product typological system: a progress report and partial evaluation', *Working Series in Marketing Research*, College of Business Administration, Penn State University, Paper No 12.

Fishbein M (1967), 'Attitude and the prediction of behaviour', in Fishbein M (ed), *Readings in Attitude and Measurement*, Wiley, New York.

Fishbein M and Ajzen I (1975) *Belief, Attitude: Intention and Behaviour*, Addison-Wesley, Reading, Mass.

—(1980), 'Predicting and understanding consumer behaviour: attitude-behaviour correspondence', in Ajzen I and Fishbein M (eds) *Understanding Attitudes and Predicting Social Behaviour*, Prentice-Hall, Englewood Cliffs NJ.

Foxall G R (1990), *Consumer Psychology in Behavioural Perspective*, Routledge, London.

Krech D and Crutchfield R S (1962), *Individual in Society*, McGraw-Hill, New York.

Krugman H E (1965), 'The impact of television advertising: learning without involvement', *Public Opinion Quarterly*, 29, pp 349–55.

—(1967), 'Memory without recall, exposure without perception', *Journal of Advertising Research*, 17 (4), pp 7–12.

Levitt T (1970), 'The morality (?) of advertising', *Harvard Business Review*, 48, pp 84–92.

Marketing Week (1986), an interview with R Foulsham of the BSN Group, 8 July.

Mintel (1988), *Fruit Juices and Mineral Water*, Aug, pp 3–14.

Ryan M A and Bonfield E H (1980), 'Fishbein's intentions model, a test of external and pragmatic validity', *Journal of Marketing*, 44 (2), pp 82–95.

Sampson P and Harris P (1970), 'A users guide to Fishbein', *Journal of the Market Research Society*, 12 (3), pp 145–66.

Source Perrier (1987), verbatim comments by the CEO of Leo Burnett (UK) in Perrier promotional literature.

Thompson F (1986), 'The mineral water market', *Financial Times*.

Tuck M (1973), 'Fishbein theory and the Bass-Talarzyk problem', *Journal of Marketing Research*, 19, pp 345–48.

Wilkie W (1986), *Consumer Behaviour*, Wiley, New York.

Wilson D T, Mathews H L and Harvey J W (1975), 'An empirical test of the Fishbein behavioural intention model', *Journal of Consumer Research*, 1 (4), pp 39–48.

6

BRAND PRICING IN A RECESSION[*]

Leslie de Chernatony, Simon Knox

and Mark Chedgey

OUTLINE

In the UK packaged grocery market, multiple grocery retailers are often in a far more powerful negotiating position than many brand manufacturers. Pressure has historically been exerted on the weaker manufacturers to reduce consumer support for their brands, in favour of extra discounts for retailers. Weaker players acquiesced to these demands trying to compete on lower prices. With a notable increase in multiple retailers' media support, and decreasing investment in manufacturer media activity, questions are raised about the extent to which consumers perceive brands as having sufficient added values to justify a price premium. In fact, do consumers perceive greater price differences between manufacturer brands and retailer brands in situations of greater manufacturer media support?

A literature review indicates that consumers show limited awareness of packaged grocery prices. However, upon being presented with a reference price, for a particular product field, consumers appear to have a greater accuracy of price recall.

In a recessionary period, we wondered whether these historical findings about consumers' knowledge of brand pricing were still valid. We sought to evaluate consumers' price recall of brands in product fields where media activity was either continually increasing or decreasing.

Brands in the still mineral water market were selected as these received continual media support. The pure orange juice market has experienced continual cuts in media activity, making this suitable for this research.

Consumer interviews were undertaken in 1990, with 80 consumers completing the mineral water study and 86 the fruit juice study. In each product field consumer awareness of correct prices of either

---

[*] This chapter first appeared in the *European Journal of Marketing*, Vol 26, No 2, 1992. © MCB University Press Ltd.

manufacturers' brands or retailers' brands was very low. When given a benchmark, consumer price recall improved with the price brand tested. Due to the poor level of price accuracy, we were unable to draw firm inferences about the impact of media support on perceptions of price differences between manufacturer and retailer brands. Managerial implications are drawn at the end of the chapter.

INTRODUCTION

In the UK packaged grocery sector, multiple retailer power continues to grow. In the ten-year period to 1988, retailers' share grew from 58 per cent to 74 per cent, with the top five retailers accounting for 62 per cent of these sales (Jorro 1991). Not only are the major multiples able to exert considerable buying power over manufacturers of branded groceries, but they have also continued to invest in their own-label ranges (Beaumont 1989). The multiples' own-label share of packaged groceries is 33 per cent and is forecast to grow to 40 per cent during the 1990s (*The Economist* 1988). In much the same way that manufacturers have traditionally communicated the values of their individual brands through advertising, retailers are now investing heavily in corporate image building by promoting the company brand to consumers (King 1991). Tesco was the leading advertiser amongst the multiples spending £13.4 million promoting the Tesco brand in 1989. None of the five major grocery multiple retailers spent less than £5.5 million during that year and Tesco, Sainsbury and Asda were amongst the top 100 advertisers (Advertising Association 1991).

Whilst the top grocery brand manufacturers consistently invest more in advertising at the company level (Proctor and Gamble was the top advertiser in 1989 with a £53.9 million spend), the promotional spend is spread across a wide portfolio of brands. Furthermore, it is diluted by media inflation that is significantly higher than the RPI. For a small number of grocery brands such as Persil, Kelloggs Cornflakes and Kitkat, consumer preferences and loyalties remain strong. However, for secondary brands, consumer preferences have been eroded as perceived values fade over time and brand commitment dwindles. In addition, primary brand manufacturers are very aware that the basis of competition has shifted; no longer can retailer own labels be regarded as a poor alternative to brands (de Chernatony 1987). However, not all brand manufacturers accept this premise and still believe that by cutting brand advertising in favour of retailer discounts, they can continue to compete successfully (Schroer 1990). An assumption implicit in this strategy is that gradual reductions in brand advertising do not adversely affect a brand's ability to sustain a price premium over competing own labels.

We explore this assumption later in the chapter since our study has been designed to test whether consumers' perceptions of the price premium which brands can sustain over own labels varies according to the levels of advertising support.

In the current recessionary climate, it has become increasingly common to see brand manufacturers promoting on price (Hoggan 1990). If a low-price strategy is to be competitive, it will only be viable if consumers are cognisant of brand prices. Thus, a second objective of our study has been to carry out a comparative assessment of price recall across grocery brands and own labels amongst UK consumers.

In the first section, we consider in more detail the role of advertising in creating brand values and propose the first research hypothesis.

ADVERTISING AND BRAND VALUES

Brands, as King (1970) explains, are preferred by consumers because they have added-values over and above commodities. When relevant added-values are recognised, consumers are prepared to pay a premium price. The nature of a brand's added-values will vary and can be as simple as the polite style of a shop assistant or as complex as the psychological values associated with buying a brand of drink that has come to signify membership of a particular social group (de Chernatony and McDonald 1992). The cluster of added-values associated with a brand depends on the degree of integration, consistency and focus of the marketing programme for that brand. For example, consistent high quality allays any concern about functional capability whilst a wide distribution base facilitates purchasing convenience. However, it is the promotional activity behind the brand which not only communicates these added-values but, in some cases, can be the prime added-value component. For example, the creative approach behind the Martini campaign, characterised by a now-familiar tone and musical refrain, all reinforce the added-value of temporary escapism to an aspirational lifestyle.

As the brand's added-values become more recognised and appreciated, consumers are increasingly able to personify the brand (Gardner and Levy 1955). The brand's character becomes more clearly defined through user experience and consistent promotional support.

However, it should not be thought that only successful manufacturers' brands provide added-values. Euromonitor (1989) showed that consumer confidence in the quality of own labels had grown to the extent that 70 per cent of consumers disagreed with the statement 'own labels tend to be poorer quality than branded goods'. Besides the added-value of quality reassurance, retailers' own labels have also developed strong personalities. This is due both to a clear store image as well as their commitment to design and advertising (Burnside 1990).

Doyle (1989) argues that brands succeed through communicating their added-values to consumers. In an earlier study, Broadbent (1979) showed that the advertising share of leading grocery brands was, in fact, in excess of their market share. Furthermore, these advertised brand leaders were all priced at a premium. Whitaker (1983), and more recently Wills and Mueller (1989) have also drawn similar conclusions about the characteristic of brands; the evidence suggests that successful brands require a significant advertising commitment to maintain a price premium. Yet, despite this, some brand manufacturers have cut advertising support either to fund bigger discounts to retailers or to make better short-term profits (Jones 1986). In such situations, consumers are increasingly likely to shift their allegiance from these weakly supported brands to the equivalent own label. As sales fall over time, retailers will then demand additional support to stock the brand. When brand margins become squeezed in this way, promotional investment is likely to be further reduced, leaving the consumer even more perplexed as to why they should pay a premium (de Chernatony 1989). To test this central proposition, we developed our first hypothesis for empirical validation:

- H1: in product fields where advertising support for manufacturers' brands has increased over time, consumers will perceive a noticeable price difference between these brands and own labels; where advertising support has been in continual decline, consumers will not perceive a noticeable price differential.

The remaining two research hypotheses are discussed in the next section which also addresses the literature on consumer perceptions of price, product-quality evaluation and the shift in this relationship due to price-based competition.

CONSUMERS' PERCEPTIONS OF PRICE AND QUALITY

The early researchers investigating the relationship between price and perceived quality (eg McConnell 1968) conducted their studies by allowing *only* price information to vary. They showed a positive price-perceived quality relation. However, to reflect market conditions more accurately, later studies allowed other parameters besides price to vary (eg Wheatley and Chiu, 1977). While there are inconsistencies in these results, the meta-analysis by Monroe (1990) broadly supports the notion of a positive price-perceived quality relationship. Thus, if noticeable price reductions occur amongst manufacturers' brands competing on price, it is possible that consumers may actually perceive a concomitant reduction in product quality!

The second questionable assumption associated with price reduction is that consumers know the actual prices of products. Several studies have shown that this may not be the case. In fact, there is evidence of consumers' buying intentions being influenced more by relative, rather than absolute, prices (Monroe 1977).

With regard to absolute recall of grocery product prices, Gabor (1988) reports the results of longitudinal research which clearly shows a marked deterioration in price recall amongst consumers. For example, 84 per cent were able to state the correct price of tea in 1958 while, in 1984, only 53 per cent could do so to within a price band of ± 10p. These findings are not unique to the UK; Gabor also shows from *Progressive Grocer* publications that correct price recall has also fallen over time in the USA.

In a separate study, McGoldrick and Marks (1986) questioned shoppers immediately after they had paid for their packaged groceries and discovered that only 29 per cent were able to recall prices correctly. Similarly, *The Grocer* (1988) reported that only 16 per cent correctly recalled the price of Heinz Baked Beans.

It is evident that consumers' price awareness of grocery products has fallen. In recessionary times, we felt it important that a more up-to-date study should be completed, given the increased incidence of low-price competition. Based on the literature review, we anticipated that a low level of price recall would still prevail but felt that, with a reference price to evaluate competing offerings, the accuracy of recall would increase. Specifically our second hypothesis states:

- H2: consumers show a limited price awareness of competing grocery products within a price band (± 10p of the actual store price) but, with a reference price, there would be a marked increase in the accuracy of recall within the price band.

Further, in product fields where advertising support has been maintained, the literature suggests that consumers are likely to perceive more added-values for brands than in sectors where advertising activity has been cut. Given a positive price-perceived quality relationship, we posit our third hypothesis:

- H3: consumers are likely to overestimate the price of manufacturers' brands in product fields that have benefited from increased advertising support, and to underestimate brand prices in product fields subjected to reduced advertising over time.

METHODOLOGY

Product fields and brands investigated

Initially, 15 grocery product fields were screened using the following criteria for selection:

- The sector should be supported by a real increase, or decrease, in advertising support over the seven-year period to 1989, as measured using MEAL data
- The sector should have wide grocery distribution and high household penetration
- The sector should have a multiple brand/own-label presence and a standard pack size across both categories

Two product fields satisfied these criteria. The first was mineral water to represent the continuously increasing advertised sector, with a 720 per cent *increase* in spend over the period. The second was fruit juices where advertising had been consistently reduced. In fact it fell by 60 per cent* over the period.

In the £200 million mineral water market, sparkling water accounted for 55 per cent and still waters for 45 per cent of sales during 1989. However, in the sparkling sector there had recently been a highly publicised contamination scare which we felt may have heightened brand and price awareness and certainly reduced the availability of the leading brand, Perrier. For these reasons, we focused on the still water sector. Evian, Buxton and Highland Spring were selected as these were the main brands in 2 litre pack sizes. In the fruit juice market, pure orange was found to be the dominant variety and the 1 litre pack the dominant size. Again, the three leading brands were selected on this basis: Del Monte, Princes and Sun Pride. Interviewing took place in London suburbs where Sainsbury, Tesco and Safeway stores are common. All the manufacturers' brands were stocked by these multiple retailers. So, in total, three brands and three own-label products were used in both tests.

It is interesting to note that in the strongly advertised mineral water

---

* Deflated MEAL figures based on 1985 prices.

market Evian, as brand leader, had a 19 per cent share with own labels at 26 per cent. Yet, in the reduced-advertising fruit juice market, the brand leader Del Monte only had a 10 per cent market share while own labels had 63 per cent; prima-facie evidence in support of the role of advertising in enhancing the added-value positioning of brands.

Data collection

A series of in-home interviews were completed in the second half of 1990 using a fully structured questionnaire. The questionnaire was designed to elicit consumers' perceptions of competing brands' prices and had been piloted prior to the survey. Respondents were recruited only if they had bought and drunk one of the six competing brands (either orange juice or mineral water) within the past four weeks and were primarily responsible for buying household groceries. Subsequently, they were only questioned about one of the product fields. In total, 80 interviews were conducted amongst mineral water consumers and 86 amongst fruit juice consumers. For each product field, the samples were split approximately equally between male and female and across age profiles which broadly matched the market (Mintel 1990 a,b).

Initially, respondents were shown packs of each of the six competing brands in the product field and were asked how much they thought each would cost (without revealing any price cues). Subsequently, respondents were then told the actual store price of the brand leader in the product field (65p for Evian and 89p for Del Monte) and asked again how much each of the remaining brands and own labels cost. The questionnaires were then analysed using the SPSS suite of programs on the basis of accurate price recall (H1, H3) and within the ± 10p price band (H2).

RESULTS

Price differentials and advertising support

There was no price variation between the three chains' prices for each of the manufacturers' brands (their in-store prices are shown in the Appendix). The actual price of the mineral water brands always exceeded that of own labels with an average price premium of 22 per cent. In contrast, within the fruit juice market, the Tesco and Safeway own labels were priced higher than the brands. The average price differential of brands over own labels was only 1 per cent. These observations support the literature review, that strongly advertised brands can more readily sustain a price premium at store level.

Table 6.1 Perceived and actual price differentials

Market (Change in advertising)		Mineral water (Supported)	Fruit juices (Cut)
1. Mean perceived prices (no reference price)			
	Brand (p)	72.3	80.0
	Own Label (p)	62.7	70.0
Perceived price premium (%)		15.3%	14.3%
Actual price premium (%)		22.0%	1.0%
2. Mean perceived prices (Reference price of brand leader given)			
	Brand (p)	61.5	80.0
	Own Label (p)	55.3	71.7
Perceived price premium (%)		11.2%	11.6%
Actual price premium (%)		11.8%	(2.8%)

However, our interest was in evaluating whether consumers' *perceptions* of these price differentials was consistent with the actual pricing patterns in-store. In Table 6.1, our results show that, without a reference price, the perceived price differential was 15.3 per cent for mineral water brands and 14.3 per cent for the fruit juice brands, neither of which is in accord with the actual price premiums at point of purchase. Given a reference price, the perceived price differential in the mineral water sector was reduced to 11.2 per cent; a differential which was remarkably similar to the 11.6 per cent observed for the fruit juice brands.

In view of there being no significant differences in the perceived price differentials between brands and own labels across either product field, *hypothesis H1 is rejected.* We do not believe these results imply that advertising is ineffective in reinforcing brands' added-values; it is more likely that they reflect consumers' inability to recall brand prices accurately, as the next section of this chapter shows. In fact, in view of the earlier literature review suggesting consumers judge prices on a relative, rather than absolute basis, it may have been better to ask consumers to evaluate the extent to which they perceive price differentials between brands and own labels.

The accuracy of price recall

Table 6.2 highlights the percentage of consumers with accurate price recall under the test conditions. In general, consumers showed very limited ability to recall absolute prices across either product categories, which confirms the results of earlier studies. For example, only 15 per cent correctly recalled the price of the leading mineral water brand (Evian) and 6 per cent in the fruit juice sector (Del Monte). Not unexpectedly, a higher proportion of consumers were able to estimate prices within ± 10p of the actual price. However, still only 59 per cent of consumers were able to do this for Evian (66 per cent for Del Monte).

Interestingly, the results also indicate that price awareness varied considerably between competing brands and own labels, irrespective of market share.

Once the price of the brand leader in the product field had been made known, there was still a lot of uncertainty about the prices of the remaining products. There was no evident improvement in the proportion of consumers able to judge prices correctly. However, by relaxing price recall accuracy to within ± 10p of the actual price there was a noticeable shift. For each of the brands, and some own labels, there was a very marked improvement in the percentage of consumers able to

Table 6.2 Price perceptions

Mineral water	Evian %	Buxton %	H. Spring %	Sainsbury %	Tesco %	Safeway %
1. Correct price recall (no reference price)	15	3	5	–	1	1
± 10p	59	36	56	39	57	37
2. Correct price recall (reference price of brand leader given)		1	5	–	4	1
± 10p		84	90	70	93	67

Fruit juices	Del Monte %	Princes %	Sun Pride %	Sainsbury %	Tesco %	Safeway %
1. Correct price recall (no reference price)	6	1	6	–	2	1
± 10p	66	68	72	59	34	32
2. Correct price recall (with reference pricing)		–	8	–	4	2
± 10p		91	87	74	41	39

estimate prices within the band. For mineral water brands, over 80 per cent were now able to gauge within ± 10p, whilst for own-label products, the proportion rose to 67 per cent or more. For fruit juice brands, the figure was very similar to mineral water with 87 per cent (or more) of consumers gauging correctly within the price band. However, for own-label fruit juices the improvement in recall was less evident, particularly for the Tesco and Safeway products.

From these results H2 can be accepted; consumers show limited ability to correctly recall absolute prices, even within a price band of ± 10p. However, once benchmarked, recall within the same price band improved considerably. Judgements about prices appear to be based more on the relative prices of competing products rather than absolute prices, even in times of recession.

The impact of advertising support on price perceptions

We argued in H3 that, when considering the price perceptions of manufacturers' brands, consumers would be more likely to overestimate the price of brands in strongly advertised product fields and to underestimate prices if advertising had been reduced. Our analysis of these pricing perceptions is shown in Table 6.3. When consumers are least sure of brand prices (ie without a reference price), they showed a consistent bias towards *overestimation* of the prices of mineral water brands. In contrast, for the fruit juices, the majority of consumers consistently tended to *underestimate* the price of manufacturers' brands in the absence of a reference price. *These findings support H3.*

Without reference pricing, consumers show great uncertainty about brand prices and rely upon brand names to recall brand values. With a continuing advertising presence, it is easier for consumers to associate brand names with added-values; as advertising is withdrawn consumers appear to find it increasingly hard to recall these values over time. In the former situation, brand prices are overestimated as brands can be differentiated, whilst in the latter case, brand prices are underestimated and brands undifferentiated. In fact, when reference prices were given, we found that this relationship did not hold because of a suspected interaction between consumers' original price expectation and the reference price which affected their basis for price judgement.

The managerial implications of our findings are discussed in more detail in the concluding section.

Table 6.3   Price perceptions of brands

| | Mineral water | | |
	Evian	Buxton	H. Spring
Overestimate (%)	68	85	68
Correct (%)	15	3	5
Underestimate (%)	17	12	27
	Fruit Juice		
	Del Monte	**Princes**	**Sun Pride**
Overestimate (%)	38	34	30
Correct (%)	6	1	6
Underestimate (%)	56	65	64

CONCLUSIONS

In a recessionary period characterised by increasing retailer power, it has become more common for brand manufacturers to compete through price promotion and by cutting advertising support. As the level of brand investment is eroded, so too are the added-values that distinguished between brands. In such situations, consumers are increasingly likely to shift their allegiance to the equivalent own labels which, in turn, are now able to compete very successfully with brands at the functional and psycho-social level.

The empirical aspect of the research described in this chapter has been the comparison of consumer price perceptions in two distinct grocery markets: one characterised by increasing advertising support and the other in decline.

Consumer awareness of correct prices of either brands or own labels was very low indeed. For example, only 6 per cent could correctly state the price of Del Monte, the brand leader in a £960 million market. One-third of consumers were not even able to estimate the price of this brand to within ± 10p. So brand promotion strategies that feature low-price announcements are ineffective. Further, the lack of awareness of own-label prices implies that retailers have been successful in repositioning their offerings so that they compete on the same terms as established brands with less dependency on low price to differentiate. However, our research shows that a brand price differential still exists in the minds of consumers when prompted to think in these terms. In-store, retailers are trying to shift these perceptions by closing the premium gap where own-label and brand differentiation has been eroded.

When given a benchmark, consumer price recall improved within the price band that was tested. Clearly, in today's trading conditions, price promotions should be communicated relative to either the original price or a competitor. We have also concluded that low pricing, even with a reference price, may run the risk of low consumer impact if contained within the 10p discount range (ie 12–15 per cent reduction in the original price) since the trend has been away from price-based purchasing behaviour. On the other hand, if the price cut is made too deep, consumers may interpret this as an erosion in quality if perceived to be outside the region of price 'acceptability'. We would strongly recommend that manufacturers reassess this pivotal position in consumer tests so that the correct balance can be struck if price promotion is deemed the preferred tactical option. However, we do not believe that low-price promotion provides a sustainable long-term strategy.

Finally, there is clear evidence from the research that mineral water manufacturers may not be pricing aggressively enough against the levels of advertising investment. It would appear that for these manufacturers, their brand names evoke added-values that reinforce a positive price-perceived quality relationship which lead consumers to overestimate brand prices. Manufacturers must be ready to close this perceived value gap by appropriate price increase. It would seem to us in the retailers' interest to facilitate such increases since they, in turn, could readily increase the price of their own-label mineral waters.

It would be inappropriate to draw too many broader conclusions from this research as the scope is limited. However, we do seek to reopen the question about how marketing management determines the price of their grocery brands and own labels in relation to competition, perceived quality and market structures. Our evidence suggests that a positive price-quality relationship still exists where marketing management has the courage to continue supporting brands in times of recession and media stagflation. As a quid pro quo they must also have the courage and skill to negotiate price increases based on consumer-perceived value.

Appendix 1

Increased advertising support: mineral water

	Actual price (p)	Mean perceived price (p)	Mean price (p) perceived when told Evian cost 65p
Evian	65	74	
Buxton	56	72	62
Highland Spring	62	71	61
Average brand price	**61.0**	**72.3**	**61.5**
Sainsbury own label	49	63	56
Tesco own label	53	63	55
Safeway own label	48	62	55
Average own-label price	**50.0**	**62.7**	**55.3**

Reduced advertising support: Fruit Juice

	Actual price (p)	Mean perceived price (p)	Mean price (p) perceived when told Del Monte cost 89p
Del Monte	89	85	
Princes	81	80	82
Sun Pride	79	75	78
Average brand price	**83.0**	**80.0**	**80.0**
Sainsbury own label	77	72	73
Tesco own label	85	69	71
Safeway own label	85	69	71
Average own-label price	**82.3**	**70.0**	**71.1**

REFERENCES

Advertising Association (1991), *Marketing Pocket Book*, Advertising Association, London.

Beaumont J (1989), 'Grocery retailing in the 1990s', *Retail and Distribution Management*, Nov/Dec, pp 9–12.

Broadbent S (1979), 'What makes a top brand?' *Nielson Researcher*, 3, pp 1–13.

Burnside A (1990), 'Package Deal', *Marketing*, 15, Feb, pp 29–30.

de Chernatony L (1987), 'Consumers' Perceptions of the Competitive Tiers in Six Grocery Markets', unpublished PhD thesis, City University Business School, London.

—L (1989), 'Branding in an Era of Retailer Dominance', *International Journal of Advertising*, 8 (3), pp 245–60.

de Chernatony L and McDonald M (1992), *Creating Powerful Brands*, Butterworth Heinemann, Oxford.

Doyle, P. (1989), 'Building Successful Brands: the Strategic Options', *Journal of Marketing Management*, 5 (1), pp 77–95.

Economist The (1988), 'Label Wars', 16 April, p 84.

Euromonitor (1989), *UK Own Brands*, Euromonitor, London.

Gabor A (1988), *Pricing*, Gower, Aldershot.

Gardner M and Levy SJ (1955), 'The Product and the Brand', *Harvard Business Review*, 33, Mar–Apr, pp 33–9.

Grocer The (1988), '10,000 customers prove how little they care about grocers' prices', 27, Aug, p 5.

Hoggan K (1990), 'Desperate Measures', *Marketing*, 13 Dec, pp 22–3.

Jones P (1986), *What's in a Name?*, Lexington Books, Lexington.

Jorro R (1991), 'Heat is on for the Top Retail Spot', *Supermarketing*, 18th Jan, p 1.

King S (1970), *What is a Brand?*, J W Thompson, London.

—(1991), 'Brand Building in the 1990s', *Journal of Marketing Management*, 7 (1), pp 3–13.

Mintel (1990a), *Mineral Waters*, May, Mintel Publications Ltd, London.

—(1990b), *Fruit Juices*, July, Mintel Publications Ltd, London.

McConnell J (1968), 'The Price Quality Relationship in an Experimental Setting', *Journal of Marketing Research*, 5 (3), pp 300–3.

McGoldrick P and Marks H (1986), 'How Many Grocery Prices do Shoppers Really Know?', *Retail and Distribution Management*, 14 (1), pp 24–7.

Monroe K (1977), 'Objective and Subjective Contextual Influence on Price Perception', in Woodside A, Sheth J and Bennett P (eds), *Consumer and Industrial Buying Behavior*, North Holland Publishing Company, Amsterdam.

Monroe K (1990), *Pricing*, McGraw-Hill, New York.

Schroer J (1990), 'Ad Spending: Growing Market Share', *Harvard Business Review*, Jan–Feb, pp 44–8.

Wheatley J and Chiu J (1977), 'The Effects of Price, Store Image and Product and Respondent Characteristics on Perceptions of Quality', *Journal of Marketing Research*, 14, May, pp 181–6.

Whitaker J (1983), 'To spend or not to spend?', *Nielson Researcher*, 2, pp 1–15.

Wills R and Mueller W (1989), 'Brand Pricing and Advertising', *Southern Economic Journal*, 56 (2), pp 383–95.

PART TWO

MANAGING CONSUMER MARKETS

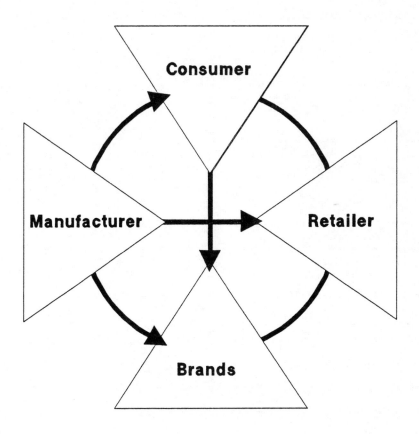

7

BRAND BUILDING AND MARKET RESEARCH*

Stephen King

OUTLINE

Marketing companies face formidable pressures in the 1990s: more confident and individualistic consumers demanding higher quality and 'real values'; new technology accelerating change; increasing international competition. The key skill they will need to meet the pressures will be brand building – the creation of ever-improving, unique, desirable entities. But the brand building will be in many ways different from that featured in most textbooks, which are firmly based on the classic product brands – Coke, Pepsi, Marlboro, Lux Toilet Soap, Bovril and so on.

Brand building will be entering a new mode, in which the norm will be the company brand. That is, the brand discriminator will be not so much product attributes as people's skills, attitudes, behaviour, style and responsiveness: in fact, the whole company culture. In its turn this will mean that the service element inherent in any brand will become increasingly important.

The staff in any company will gradually be seen as the main brand builder and the brand's most important medium of communication. The implications of this are far reaching, and affect the formation and dissemination of strategy; organisation and structure; corporate culture; how consumer problems are solved; the role of the personnel department; training, motivation and rewards; and internal communications.

Brand building is clearly far more complex when the brand is the company, and so are the tasks for market research. Researchers will have to deal with a wider variety of respondents, who can have various relationships with the brand. They will have to understand and evaluate

---

* Presented at a Market Research Society seminar in London, 26 February 1991. Reprinted with the kind permission of the Market Research Society.

the more intangible elements of service and company culture. They will have to communicate complex phenomena and mathematical concepts in simple language. Like marketers, they will have to adjust to a world in which the triggers of marketing success are not things but people.

INTRODUCTION

There are two major evolutionary changes in the nature of marketing that are greatly affecting market research at present. The chapter covers:

- The special pressures affecting brand building
- The two evolutionary changes
- The implications for market research methods.

The early parts of the chapter are in effect a summary, as I have written about the same area at length elsewhere (King 1991). Equally, I will not be dealing directly with the development of research company brands, which has been well covered before (eg Bowles 1991; Whitten 1991).

SIX PRESSURES ON MARKETING COMPANIES

There are six particular pressures that have grown steadily through the 1980s and are likely to intensify:

- *More confident consumers.* People are more confident, readier to experiment and to trust their own judgement. There is more individualism and tribalism, more know-how, more understanding of all aspects of marketing. There will be a cooler analysis of the values given by brands, products and services; and maybe a more critical approach to some forms of research.

- *New concepts of 'quality'.* Consumers will continue to look for quality, but their interpretation of it is changing. It is increasingly based on what they feel are *real values* – not superficial styling. They will be more interested in values such as responsiveness, service and greenism, and will be willing to pay a little extra for a clear conscience. That is, demand will become more complex, and so will the measurement of it.

- *Shortage of skills.* Demographic changes and educational weaknesses may mean a shortage of the skills needed to invent and produce these high-quality goods and services, to manage all aspects of their marketing and to plan their research.

- *Increased competition.* Competition is intensifying in almost all fields and is becoming more international. It is clear that there will soon be considerable over-capacity in many markets – for instance cars, retailing and financial services.

- *The side-effects of new technology.* However much we have all talked about new technology, progress on using it in marketing has been a bit slow. But that will surely change in the 1990s. There will be more rapid copying of goods, more flexible manufacturing systems, more automation of services, faster technological leapfrogging, shorter lifecycles. The database revolution will at last actually happen. Retailers will make use of their scanning data not just for stock control and arm-wrestling with their suppliers, but also for building a closer relationship with their customers.

- *Restructuring.* The wave of mergers, takeovers, LBOs, MBOs, corporate alliances, bundling, unbundling and barbarians at the gates shows little sign of slowing down. Many organisations and employees will be wondering who they are, to whom they owe loyalty and what their corporate culture is. Customers will be wondering just how committed to their brands some of the suppliers really are.

All these changes will make life difficult for companies. How will they keep up their margins in the face of stronger international competition? How will they make the most of economies of scale when national mass-markets are being broken up into transnational tribes? How will they attract the skills to keep ahead on quality? If they are being constantly restructured, how will they build an enduring link with their customers?

Most people in marketing (eg Doyle 1989) would agree that building and maintaining powerful brands will be critical to success. Indeed, brand building may be the *only* way in these circumstances to get stability of demand, to add the values and variants that people want, to provide a base for expansion, to protect the company against the power of intermediaries and to attract the right staff.

This is hardly a new idea. Building brands is at the centre of all marketing. The trouble is that we tend to equate the word 'brand' with the classic brand leaders in packaged grocery products (such as Coke, Pepsi, Marlboro, Ivory, Persil, Lux Toilet Soap, Oxo, Bovril, Kit Kat, Mars, Andrex). Yet one effect of the pressures of the 1990s will be that, though the old-established classic brands should themselves prosper, this sort of brand will become steadily rarer and a smaller part of consumers' expenditure. We are going to have to get out of the habit of using the old classic brands as the 'true' model for marketing.

I believe, in fact, that brand building is entering a new mode. This is partly because of the speed and scale of today's pressures. But it is also because the long-promised 'service economy' seems genuinely to have arrived at last. White-collar work is now the employment mode of the majority in developed economies, and people are increasingly getting their rewards from the non-functional aspects of brands.

TWO EVOLUTIONARY CHANGES

There are two interlocking elements to this new mode – the two major evolutionary changes to marketing in the 1990s:

- The company brand itself will increasingly become the discriminator in consumers' choice, rather than the functional attributes of objects made by the company.
- Almost everything we buy is a combination of 'product' and 'service'. The service element will steadily become the more important part, and the principles of service marketing will become the core of all brand building.

The company brand

Successful new single-line brands have gradually become something of a rarity (Madell 1980; Tauber 1988). Most successful new products are range extensions or line extensions – that is, they are variants of an existing brand. Each variant is rapidly matched or trumped by a competitor or a retailer; and still the new individualists demand more variety.

The result is a tendency to stretch a successful product brand to cover fields some way from its original (product) values. When this happens, consumers will often 'invent' a parent company to own both the new variant and the original brand – the variant is seen as a new product from 'the Nescafé people' or 'the Timotei people' – and they will assume certain company values for both.

So it seems that the company brand (whether technically it is a company, like Heinz, or a presumed company, like 'the Timotei people') will cover an increasingly wider range of product types and the brand will not credibly be able to convey that all its products are always 'better' than its competitors'.

This implies that increasingly the company brand itself will act as the main discriminator. That is, consumers' choice will depend less on an evaluation of the functional benefits to them of a product or service, more on an assessment of the people behind it – their skills, attitudes, integrity, behaviour, style, responsiveness, greenism, language: the whole company culture, in fact.

Company brands have of course been around a very long time, even in the world of packaged groceries. But it seems to me that most of the emphasis in the literature and teaching and conferences is still on the single-line classic brand. The change has in fact been quite rapid. For instance, as recently as 1969, of the 25 brands spending most on press and television in the UK (MEAL data), 19 were repeat-purchase packaged goods; by 1989 it was just one and in 1990 two.

I wonder if we have quite come to grips yet with this change. The differences between company brands and the classic (product) brands, though fairly obvious, have some important implications for both marketing and research. To pick out four such differences:

- *The consumers have changed.* Most of the classic brands were launched when authority was respected and so mass-marketing was possible. The brand became the authority in its own small world. Now everything is questioned, and people want to be treated as individuals. The company's views are not necessarily fully accepted; market research has to take this into account.
- *Copying the product element is easier.* Most of the classic brands had a good run before copies came onto the market. This is simply not so for today's company brands. Their discriminators will depend on more subtle, non-functional values – much harder to measure.
- *Relationships are more diverse.* For the classic brands, the main points of contact are retailers and consumers. For the company brand it's a much wider range of overlapping groups. This means that an individual can have several different relationships with the brand (eg consumer, employee, shareholder, pressure group member). It also means that the brand will use a much wider range of communication methods. In particular, the staff (from the CEO to the telephonist) will probably be the most important medium.
- *The core of the brand is people, not things.* Unlike the classic brand, a company brand is not a standard article. It is a changing collection of people, values, styles and behaviour. What binds them together is very intangible – a complex set of norms, conventions, methods, examples, organisational patterns, rules and leaders. It is of course extremely difficult to measure the personality of this sort of brand.

There are some broader implications from the move to company brands. For instance, if the staff become the crucial brand builders and communicators, there may have to be some changes in staff policies in many companies. Companies may have to give more attention to clarifying strategies; to the role of the personnel director in marketing; to training, motivation and leadership; to identifying and establishing a corporate culture; to improving internal networks; to internal communications in general. Where such complexities need to be improved, they will also need to be measured.

Again, the typical hierarchical family-tree type structure that works (more or less) for classic brands is likely to be unsuitable for managing and communicating a company brand. That may need a more interactive group management. It may also need a 'brand designer', a new type of animal, whose passion is for the totality of the brand (Lorenz 1986). Such a person may need to use measurement methods that straddle the gap between the traditions of market research (as used in the marketing department) and those of human resources research (as used in the personnel department).

The increased complexities of the target groups and media used for a company brand mean that there is a special need for clarity in setting communication objectives, in a language that is shared between several departments with several budgets and often large numbers of (competing) outside agencies and suppliers. This is a far harder task than for the classic brands (Booms and Bitner 1981); yet in my experience it is rarely tackled as systematically. This obviously presents considerable problems for planning research to measure the effectiveness of company brand communications.

Adding services

The second evolutionary change is more directly related to the coming of the 'service economy', but is maybe a little more subtle than is often assumed. It is not merely that more of people's money will be spent on 'services' rather than on 'products'. It is more that virtually everything we buy is a combination of product and service (Foxall 1985) and that the service element will be increasingly vital to success in all brands (Christopher 1985). It will provide most of the scope for the innovation and differentiation that all good brands need (Quinn et al 1990; Vandermerwe and Rada 1988).

For instance, the archetypal manufacturer, General Motors, is said to be making more money now from financing cars than from constructing them. The computer companies in particular have changed their balance. Apple is now really a management service company which concentrates on designing its basic concepts and appearance and certain software; its chips, microprocessors, video monitors, printers and power supplies are all bought-in components. IBM now offers a 'systems-integration' service; it will make the whole set-up work, whatever brands of hardware the customer buys.

There clearly are many very successful branded services, and a good deal has been written on the subject. Nevertheless the marketing of services is *relatively* new. Most of the academic work has come in the 1970s and 1980s, and not very much of it is specifically about brand building. Some of the services that prospered in the boom are finding that their brands are not quite strong enough to stand up well to hard times. Most conferences and articles by practitioners seem to treat service marketing as a specialism rather than as a central aspect of all marketing. I think it's fair to suggest that the principles have not percolated very far yet; but that seems certain to change.

There seem to me to be six basic principles that feature in most of the literature, and all of them have implications for market research methods.

Services can be added to almost any brand

The horrid word 'servitization' has been coined to cover the broader area of goods + services + knowledge + support + self-service (Vandermerwe and Rada 1988). The opportunities seem endless. For instance:

- Adding new links in the buying system. Most things we buy are part of a long process that runs from a first trigger to the final satisfaction after use; and there are often gaps in the stages. For instance SAS moved from being just another airline to being a businessperson's 'total travel package', with initial enquiry services, hotels with their own check-in counters, tours, catering, 'sleepclass' and 'work-class' tickets and limousine service.
- Adding to the assumed lifetime of products with guarantees, insurance, updates and so on.
- Providing extra information: on how to use products and with what, health, environment effects and so on.
- Improving customers' and consumers' skills: from running cookery or driving schools to training retailers' staff.
- Defining and publicising quality standards, telling consumers and the staff what to expect; then accepting and responding to the pressure that this puts on the brand.
- Setting up extra or better contacts: hotlines, ombudspeople, named contacts, 24 hour answerphones, newsletters, properly designed and maintained databases.
- Friendly delivery systems. For instance, many heating companies just

Percent rating most important:

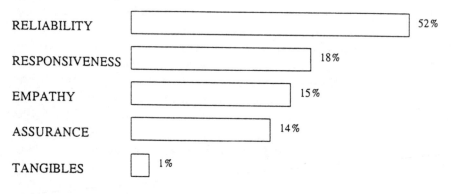

Figure 7.1 Service/quality dimensions: customers in four service sectors

used to deliver fuel to order; now they have automatic refuelling systems, boiler maintenance, spare parts, insurance etc.
• Contributing to the local community.

It's not too hard to have ideas for added services. The problem is to work out which would have sufficient appeal to differentiate the brand and to justify their extra cost. To do that will require having much more knowledge about customers', and consumers' experience, attitudes and behaviour in a much wider context than is usually necessary for a classic product brand. There seems to be a good opportunity for market researchers of the consultant rather than the 'standardised' sort and for great ingenuity in controlling the costs of such research.

The intangible elements of services are more valued than the tangible

There are many problems in measuring the quality of a service; yet it is critical if the service element of a company brand is its main discriminator. Many writers make the point that any service is made up of tangibles and intangibles, and that generally the intangibles are the more important to customers (Lovelock 1983; Thompson, DeSouza and Gale 1985). For instance, research among customers for credit cards, repairs, long-distance telephones and banks (Berry et al 1988) showed these results. (Figure 7.1)

It appeared that the physical facilities, equipment and appearance of staff mattered a lot less than reliable performance and various aspects of the relationship with customers. Many readers of this report might quarrel with the research method used, but all would admit that there are considerable problems of definition and measurement of intangibles in assessing the quality of service.

Services are the key to customer retention

For years the rhetoric of marketing has been that of warfare (targets, campaigns and offensives); the macho approach is to beat the enemy and win new customers. Now at last more attention is being paid to retaining customers, the lifetime value of a customer and 'zero defections'. Bain & Company have put figures on the increasing profits from each year of retention of a customer over 100 companies, and they all show the same trends. Figure 7.2 gives one example (Reichheld and Sasser 1990).

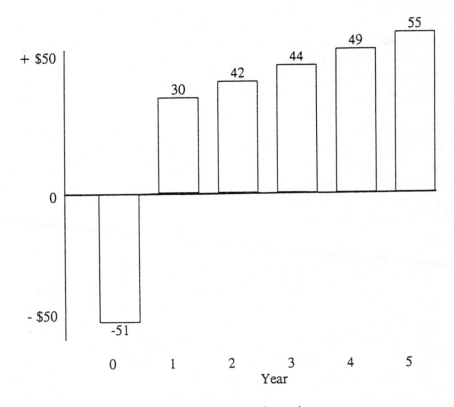

Figure 7.2 Profit from a credit card customer

Most authorities and practitioners say that added services and quality of service are the key to retaining customers (Berry 1986). BA's famous turnaround and its 'Putting people first' programme of improved service were aimed at retention. So are the various frequent flier schemes. Volvo has introduced the concept of lifetime care, a commitment to supporting the car irrespective of age or mileage.

The implications for research are fairly clear. To be effective at retention marketing a company brand has to have a really good database of present and past customers, with details of the nature of the relationship. It then has to know about the attitudes, in this difficult area of tangible and intangible service quality, of these known individuals; and if they have defected, why they have.

Internal marketing is essential

Most people, even in manufacturing companies, are doing jobs with a high service content and everyone in the company should by now be involved in total quality management. In many ways the essence of an effective service is that the employee and the customer should become accomplices in providing it (Lovelock 1984; Takeuchi and Quelch 1983).

So a key idea in all service marketing is the need to treat the staff also as customers. That implies paying a lot of attention to internal communication, motivation, reward and recognition systems. Success will depend on having just as good information on the staff as on the external market, but clearly the relationships are much more complex and sensitive. Research into staff attitudes tends to be specialised, and is on the whole done by human resources people, not market researchers. So there can be problems in linking external and internal attitudes.

The real test is problem resolution

A few things are bound to go wrong. The real test of the calibre of any service company is how well and how quickly it puts things right. It is actually possible to improve a reputation and the relationship with a customer by having problems, and then putting them right promptly, generously and stylishly.

This clearly requires having the right culture, the right systems and the right sort of organisation, usually one which has enough people to deal with the non-routine and which gives a fair amount of authority and discretion to those in direct contact with the customer (Berry 1986). The companies best at this make much use of 'brand gestures' – such as Marks

& Spencer's no-quibble exchange of goods. John Lewis' refunds of cash if found to be undersold, Mercedes' offer of technicians outside the dealers' working hours, Wachovia's 'sundown rule' (all customers' complaints to be responded to before the sun goes down). The brand gesture is a most effective symbol of the brand's attitudes, both for staff and for customers.

To make this work well the company has to have a very sensitive monitoring system. Most people do not complain directly to suppliers; but they do them far more harm by removing their custom and by talking about them to others. There is a need for research methods which concentrate on the exceptions (not the 99 per cent of cases where all goes well) and on winkling out the hidden dissatisfactions and problems.

In services, what gets measured gets done

Or, to be more sceptical about it, service quality doesn't improve unless it's measured. Speeches and exhortations do not achieve very much in their own right. Bain & Company found in a survey of chief executives that three-quarters had set up major customer quality programmes; but less than one-fifth reckoned that they had achieved tangible results from them. The reason became clear when middle managements were asked about their priorities: they rated the measurable aims (such as 'hitting plan') far higher than those hard to measure.

Standards need to be set in as specific terms as possible for the performance of services, retention of customers and the attitudes of customers. The results then have to be measured against them, and rewards and incentives related to the measures. This is clearly a difficult job, and since customer attitudes are crucial to it I would have thought that there is a great opportunity for market research skills. But I rather doubt if a great many research companies have yet got involved in this area.

IMPLICATIONS FOR MARKET RESEARCH

In general, then, it seems to me that these two evolutionary changes will bring a lot of opportunities for market research. Some of them are in areas which may be relatively unfamiliar to many market research companies. In almost all of them, dealing with company brands and service-intensive brands makes the job a great deal more complex than dealing with the classic product brands. Most will involve getting at attitudes, opinions and relationships that are both sensitive and quite individual. Nearly all will involve the measurement and monitoring of intangibles.

To take up the points made in Tim Bowles' excellent review of the issues facing the industry (Bowles 1991), I think that the proper approach in such a difficult area would be to start with top-quality tailor-made research; from that gradually to develop branded but fairly flexible services; and finally maybe set up some standardised research and monitoring systems.

I have to say, however, that I'm not wholly confident that it will all work out in that logical way. There's a danger of competition pushing us into starting with standardised research that is inevitably superficial. I think much vigilance will be called for.

It's hard to be wholly satisfied with our progress in measuring people's attitudes to and feelings about brands in the very much easier area of product brands. Some of the more awful research ideas still seem to be lingering on. For instance:

- *The ideal brand.* The ideal car would be very powerful and very economical, large for comfort and small for parking, with complex but simple specifications, full of luxury and very cheap. It's quite clear that consumers compare actual brands, and trade-off research should have killed off the ideal brand altogether. But it still rears its head in research. The ideal company seems to me an even more awful concept.

- *VALSism:* the notion that it is useful for marketing purposes to put people into watertight boxes according to their generic attitudes to life.

  The only sensible sort of segmentation of attitudes is mode or mood segmentation. For instance, in shopping, cooking and eating it is clear that there is an increasing polarisation between the fast/functional and the involved/enjoyable. But of course this is not a polarisation between different people: it's the same people in different moods or circumstances. Yet still, naive people segmentation goes on; in my view, it will be even more dangerous in the era of service-intensive company brands.

- *Surface measurement.* For instance, the belief that attitudes are whatever it is that is measured by what we choose to call 'attitude research'.

  For years we have conspired to accept that superficial 'attitude batteries' are measuring as complex a thing as an attitude, and that tracking brands on 'kind to the hands/not so kind to the hands' is telling us something special – despite the research that suggests that such responses are highly predictable and related to brand usage (Castleberry and Ehrenberg 1990). I hope we are not going to be content with tracking company brands on 'kind to employees/not so kind to employees' or 'has friendly staff/not so friendly staff'.

- *Rank-ordering attributes.* I think we are still asking respondents to rank-order the importance to them of attributes in a brand, even though it has been clear for years that they find this a very abstract task little related to real life and that the results tend greatly to overvalue functional attributes. If it is true that the intangibles in service are the most effective elements, this sort of research is going to be even more dangerous.

It seems to me that, in planning the sensitive tailor-made research that I'd envisage into people's responses to company brands, we may have to remind ourselves of some of the basic principles – such as those laid out in Mollie Tarrant's fine booklet (Tarrant 1978). Or, to repeat a *cri de coeur* of my own some years ago (King 1979):

- Find out salience before asking opinions
- Ask a wide variety of question types
- Try to be personal and concrete rather than general and abstract
- Find out what respondents feel other people think
- Use people's actions as a guide to their opinions.

SOME SPECIFIC QUESTIONS ABOUT METHODS

There are a lot of implications for market research methods dotted throughout this chapter, but let me try to pull them together by setting out some of the issues that are raised in my mind. I leave it of course to skilled practitioners to provide the answers.

Respondents

- *Complexity of roles and relationships.* With company brands people are likely to have much more varied relationships than with a single-line product brand. Will this mean more difficult/more expensive sampling; or will we have to accept the risk that, unknown to us, one relationship is being affected by another? How are we going economically to measure usage of a company brand over time, if that brand covers many product/service fields?
- *Sensitivity of staff/customer research.* Much of the research will

involve specific named people who have relationships with each other. There's a danger of the research itself affecting them. Will that mean having special interviewers, with special training? Should they have a background in human resources or anthropology?

- *Databases and direct communications.* Increasingly the company will have the names of customers and lapsed customers on a database and be used to communicating directly with these people. If so, will it want to use market research agencies at all? How can researchers develop the special skills to get themselves seen as essential consultants?

Research design

- *The intangible elements of service.* How can they be made personal and concrete enough to measure sensibly? How can the consumer language be winkled out? How can that be done while doing justice to the irreducibly intangible?

- *The complexity of communications for a company brand.* The company brand is going to be using almost all formal media for communications, plus a huge variety of speech and non-verbal signals from staff.

   The communications mix will have many different roles and timescales, and its objectives may not always be crystal clear. How can research be designed to evaluate so complex a mix?

- *Corporate culture.* No one doubts its importance in the circumstances of the 1990s. But how do we define it and establish the influences on it; hence what exactly to measure, from whom and how?

Analysis

- *Complexity versus simplicity.* Much of this chapter is about trying to measure increasingly complex phenomena, plus a few attacks on our occasional use of very superficial questions. Yet the results of our 'new' research have got to be comprehensible to and actionable by people who are not experts in mathematical analysis. Some of them will have found out the hard way that there are sometimes some very questionable assumptions hidden below a certain degree of blinding with science (for instance, in some of the regression analysis used in some market modelling). How can we find the right way of presenting complex data simply?

- *Analysis of open-ended conversations.* Many of the topics raised here require sensitive, conversational interviewing; with samples large enough to cover the variety of interests and relationships; and later monitoring of the results over time. How are we going to get the quantities without destroying the sensitivity? Will there have to be new forms of qualitative research or semi-structured research? Can new technology help over this?

General issues

- *Market research tradition versus human resources tradition.* It seems to me that there's quite a gap between the traditions, methods and gurus of the marketing department and those of the personnel department in the matter of finding things out by asking people questions. Yet a key element of the new company brands is the seamless link between the staff and the customers. How can the two traditions get together, learn from each other and avoid in-fighting? At the same time, how can market research agencies grab the new opportunities inside companies?

- *Cost.* It's easy enough to suggest improvements and changes that are likely to cost a lot of money, and I've done so. How are companies going to pay for all these extra complexities in research? How can we design research that meets the challenges without being ridiculously expensive? And how can we make the case persuasively that the necessary extra costs will be essential to the success of company brands?

Others have pointed out the changes likely in the structure and working methods of market research agencies in the 1990s. It is hard to argue with the view that more of the output will be structured and standardised, that there will be a greater emphasis on providing 'value for money' services and that the profitability of research businesses may be of more interest to distant owners than the professional skills. That might make gloomy reading for those who value craft and self-determination above all.

I am a lot less gloomy myself. I think that what I've outlined suggests that there is still enormous scope for invention, ideas and leadership from the craftspeople. The whole development of service-intensive company brands will need the classical market research skills of thinking and eliciting complex notions and interpretation and creating measurement packages, at the 'consulting' end of the spectrum. And as the changes will entail getting more deeply involved in people and their curious ways, it could be an even more rewarding job than today's.

REFERENCES

Berry L L (1986), 'Big ideas in services marketing', *Journal of Consumer Marketing* 3, 2, pp 47–51.

Berry L L, Parasuramam A and Zeithaml V A (1988), 'The service-quality puzzle', *Business Horizons*, Sep/Oct, pp 35–43.

Booms B H and Bitner M J (1981), 'Marketing strategies and organisation structures for service firms', in Donnelly J and George W R (eds), *Marketing of Services*, AMA, Chicago.

Bowles T (1991), 'Issues facing the UK research industry', *Journal of the Market Research Society*, 33, 2, pp 71–81.

Castleberry S B and Ehrenberg A S C (1990), 'Brand usage: a factor in consumer beliefs', *Marketing Research*, 1, June, pp 14–20.

Christopher M (1985), 'The strategy of customer service', in Foxall G (ed) *Marketing in the service industries*, Frank Cass, London.

Doyle P (1989), 'Building successful brands: the strategic options', *Journal of Marketing Management*, 5, 1, pp 77–95.

Foxall G (1985), Marketing is service marketing', in Foxall G (ed) *Marketing in the Service Industries*, Frank Cass, London.

King S (1979), 'Public versus private opinion', *Proceedings of the 32nd ESOMAR Congress*, Brussels.

King S (1991), 'Brand building in the 1990s', *Journal of Marketing Management*, 7, 1, pp 3–13.

Lorenz C (1986), *The Design Dimension*, Blackwell, Oxford.

Lovelock, C (1983), 'Classifying services to gain strategic marketing insights', *Journal of marketing*, 47, 2, pp 9–20.

Lovelock C (1984), *Services Marketing*, Prentice-Hall, Englewood Cliffs, NJ.

Madell J (1980), 'New products: how to succeed when the odds are against you', *Marketing Week*, 22 Feb.

Quinn J B, Doorley T L and Paquette P C (1990), 'Beyond products: Services-based strategy', *Harvard Business Review*, Mar/Apr, pp 58–67.

Reichheld F F and Sasser W E (1990), 'Zero defections: quality comes to services', *Harvard Business Review*, Sep/Oct, pp 105–11.

Takeuchi H and Quelch J A (1983), 'Quality is more than making a good product', *Harvard Business Review*, July/Aug, 139–45.

Tarrant M (1978), *Interpreting Public Attitudes*, J Walter Thompson, London.

Tauber E M (1988), 'Brand leverage: strategy for growth in a cost-control world', *Journal of Advertising Research*, Aug/Sep, pp 26–30.

Thompson P, DeSouza G and Gale B T (1985, 1988), *The Strategic Management of Service Quality*, Strategic Planning Institute, Cambridge.

Vandermerwe S and Rada J (1988), 'Servitization of business: adding value by adding services', *European Management Journal*, 6, 4, pp 314–24.

Whitten P (1991), 'Using IT to enhance the role of market research', *Journal of the Market Research Society*, 33, 2, pp 113–25.

8

BLACK & DECKER DESIGNS A RECALL*

Craig Smith, John Quelch

and Gael Simonson

Editor's note

This chapter deviates from the more general, and normative, approaches taken within this book. It is included because it provides the clarity of a specific,'real-life', situation, demonstrating that managing consumer markets is not always limited to the traditional marketing mix.

OUTLINE

On 1 December, 1988, a customer reported a fire in a Black & Decker Spacemaker Plus coffeemaker. The coffeemaker had been recently launched to praise from many quarters and was a key introduction for Black & Decker's Household Product Group (HPG). The product defect threatened Black & Decker's recently established reputation and market share gains in the small domestic appliance market. HPG senior management decided the coffeemaker should be recalled. One year later, the dedicated recall team could report an unprecedented 92 per cent return rate. As well as possibly saving lives, the recall increased customer goodwill, adding to Black & Decker brand equity when it was seriously threatened.

This chapter describes how HPG became aware of the recall requirement and how it designed and implemented a recall that created new standards and a new methodology for a difficult scenario. Key to the success of the recall was targeting each unit in the field through direct marketing; HPG chose not to make intensive use of advertising. Also

---

* Reprinted from an article written by Craig Smith, John Quelch and Gael Simonson in the Fall 1991 issue of the *Design Management Journal*, © 1991 by the Design Management Institute Press, Boston, MA, with all rights reserved.

important was the ease of product identification, supported by photos of the coffeemaker, providing consumers with a compelling incentive to return the product; openness and honesty in communications, for example, not understating the seriousness of the fire risk; and turnkey logistics for consumers and channels. Most important, was taking the recall seriously. As this chapter shows, in a well-managed recall it is possible for a firm to succeed in looking good as well as doing good.

INTRODUCTION

By mid-November 1988, everything was on track. Black & Decker was shipping all it could produce of the new Spacemaker Plus[1] home appliances, including over 80,000 coffeemakers. Christmas and gift sales looked strong. The products had won praise from many quarters. In August, the Industrial Designers Society of America bestowed its Design Excellence award on the line; the October issue of *Appliance Manufacturer* magazine named Spacemaker Plus the first-place winner in its annual competition that evaluated such issues as aesthetics, function, ease of use and engineering; and the *New York Times* commented that the units were 'making inroads in a market that swooned over Krups and Braun'.

Then, on 1 December, Black & Decker's toll-free customer service number received a call: 'My Black & Decker Spacemaker Plus coffeemaker has just set itself on fire'. Fortunately, the California caller calmly explained that the fire had been confined to the unit and that it was quickly extinguished. Since he was planning to paint his kitchen, he was not concerned about the smoke damage, but he did want a replacement coffeemaker.

A customer-driven culture

Well known for its power tools, Black & Decker Corporation traces its roots to the Baltimore machine shop opened by Duncan Black and Alonzo Decker in 1910. In 1917, their company obtained a patent on the first-ever portable power drill with a pistol grip and trigger switch. By 1988, it had become the world's largest producer of power tools, marketing products in over 100 countries and having a reputation for quality, value and innovation.

A less obvious component in this global expansion was that Black & Decker had also become a leading supplier of household products such as irons and toaster ovens. The company had acquired the General

Electric (GE) Housewares Division in 1984. The terms of the acquisition permitted Black & Decker to manufacture and market appliances under the GE name until 1987. During those transition years, the Black & Decker Household Products Group (HPG) developed a programme that successfully transferred the Black & Decker name to the GE small-appliance lines and increased market share from 27 to over 30 per cent by 1988.

As part of the GE acquisition, Black & Decker inherited the Spacemaker line, a series of popular under-the-cabinet electric appliances. In evaluating the line, however, Black & Decker determined that the items were too dark in colour, bulky and no longer competitive or unique. An integrated team of former GE and Black & Decker designers, engineers and manufacturing experts was given the mandate to completely redesign the Spacemaker products. The Spacemaker Plus coffeemaker emerged from this project. It had a 'book-shaped' water reservoir that inserted like a video cassette into the coffeemaker housing, the volume of which was kept to the rear of the cabinet to reduce the actual and perceived size. Its white colour lightened the look of the product, and an attractive thermal carafe was used to receive, store and serve the coffee, eliminating the need for a 'keep-warm plate'.

The consumer responsiveness evident in the Spacemaker Plus design project reflected a shift in emphasis in the Black & Decker culture. Under the leadership of Nolan Archibald, CEO since 1985, a more complacent manufacturing mentality in the corporation was replaced by one where 'being market-driven is more than just a catch phrase; it defines [the] entire organisation'. This sensitivity to customer needs, combined with an extensive restructuring that involved both downsizing and rationalising international design and production, generated an economic turnaround for the company. In fiscal 1988, sales were $2.28 billion, earnings $87 million and the return on equity 14.1 per cent. With this track record and with the Spacemaker Plus line described in the annual report as a 'major product highlight of 1988', the reaction to the coffeemaker fire had to be swift, protecting both customers and Black & Decker's reputation for quality.

THE FIRE INVESTIGATION

David Wildman, manager of HPG's product safety and liability group, had been alerted as soon as the fire call came in. This group had reviewed the design and arranged for testing of the Spacemaker Plus coffeemaker prototype in Black & Decker laboratories. This analysis had not revealed any fire, shock or cut hazard problems. In addition, it was corporate policy not to sell a product unless it met or exceeded the requirements established by Underwriters Laboratories (UL), an independent testing organisation. In this case, with two temperature cut-offs (TCOs) to shut the unit off in the event of overheating, the coffeemaker exceeded the UL's TCO requirements.

Wildman spoke with the California customer about potential causes of the fire and arranged for collection of the coffeemaker by a courier service. Within 24 hours, the damaged unit had arrived at HPG's Shelton, Connecticut, headquarters and the investigation had begun. Working round the clock, it was established by 3 December that the source of the fire was the coffeemaker itself and not external causes or misuse. One clue as to the precise problem came from a test where the feed from the reservoir to the heater element was clamped, starving the unit of water, which resulted in overheating in new units despite the TCOs.

Wildman contacted HPG president Dennis Heiner, then in Australia. He outlined the status of the investigation and his concern that a recall might be necessary since, under the United States Consumer Product Safety Act, a manufacturer was required to recall a product when there was knowledge of a substantial product hazard. Given the circumstances, Heiner cut his trip short and returned to Shelton.

TIME FOR A DECISION

Established in 1972, the Consumer Product Safety Commission (CPSC) is responsible for overseeing more than 100 product recalls annually. Its guidelines for determining the magnitude of a safety problem include: the nature and severity of the risk; the number of defective products and the population group exposed to the products; the environment in which the defect manifests itself; and the ways in which the product can be used or misused. In this context, HPG management's biggest concern was the likelihood of a fire occurring when the product was unattended. Both versions of the Spacemaker Plus coffeemaker operated automatically and the model with the digital clock/timer could be preset to start at some later time when users might be sleeping, out of the house, or busy with other activities.

On 5 December, Wildman informed the CPSC that there had been a fire in a Spacemaker Plus coffeemaker, that an investigation was underway and that shipments of the product had been halted. He also told the corporate legal department. The next day, there was a meeting of HPG's senior management to review the facts. It was impossible to be 100 per cent certain, but it appeared that the source of the water starvation problem could be traced to the incomplete closure of the reservoir drawer. Black & Decker had distributed 88,400 coffeemakers, most to major retailers such as Sears, Penney's and Best Products. About 35,000 units were already in the hands of consumers, and only about 10 per cent of these owners were believed to have returned the owner registration card. The corporate safety manager from Black & Decker's Towson, Maryland, headquarters had indicated that a 15 to 20 per cent return of units with consumers would probably meet the letter of the law. Analysis concluded that, with a 25 per cent consumer return rate, the out-of-pocket costs of the recall would be at least $4 million.

Heiner and his associates debated the issues. Beyond the dollar costs, the conventional understanding was that recalls were difficult to do effectively, that they increased the probability of product liability litigation, that they could damage a company's reputation and that the regulatory agencies involved could be cumbersome to deal with (indeed, the estimate was that once having notified CPSC, it could take for to six weeks to negotiate a recall programme). Yet there was never any debate about whether to recall the product. Heiner was proud of HPG's innovative products. He was also personally committed to a total quality culture that put a premium on consumer care. At the end of the discussion, he challenged his colleagues to achieve a 100 per cent return rate.

DESIGNING THE RECALL

Planning and launching the recall took thirteen days. During that time, three additional fires were reported, confirming the wisdom of the recall decision. Initially, the recall was handled by the product management team. Communications were provided by the public relations department, and the consumer assistance and information office organised the response to the recall announcement. A special freephone number was set, scripts written, agents trained to deal with customers' questions, and the company's 120 service centres advised on how to handle returns.

To maintain goodwill, to provide a strong incentive for compliance with the recall request, and to reduce the likelihood of consumers seeking a refund and buying another manufacturer's product, Heiner decided HPG would give customers a free coffeemaker when they returned the Spacemaker Plus machine to a service centre. This was in addition to receiving the replacement Spacemaker Plus product when available. At any time, consumers could request a full refund at the manufacturer's suggested retail price. As Wildman explained: 'We knew we had a problem. We wanted to turn the whole thing into a positive.'

On 15 December, 1988, notice of the recall was sent by fax or recorded post to retailers, distribution centre managers and the salesforce. Retailers were asked to pull Spacemaker Plus advertising, although they would still receive Black & Decker's contribution towards those advertisements. They could continue to display and sell other Spacemaker Plus products. Sales representatives were asked to help remove unsold units for return to Black & Decker. All Black & Decker employees were sent a memo explaining the recall and requesting they send the names and addresses of any known owners to Wildman. On 16 December, a recall letter was sent by recorded post to the 3,000 customers who had returned the owner registration cards. On 19 December, HPG was able to issue a press release announcing the voluntary recall of its two Spacemaker Plus coffeemaker models, describing the potential danger and asking owners to return the units to the nearest service centre or to call the freephone for help.

Recall information was now in the hands of customers, stores and media – including major newspapers and wire services as well as consumer and trade publications. By 8 January, 1989, however, three weeks into the programme, less than 10 per cent of the distributed units had been returned – about 800 from individuals and slightly under 8,000 from dealers. Heiner was disappointed and urged Ken Homa, HPG vice president of marketing, to find a way to improve the effectiveness of the recall.

The search for alternatives

Homa and Gael Simonson, HPG director of brand marketing and strategy development, had already been exploring other options. One significant change was deciding that the recall had to be managed by a specially established team that would have clear 'ownership' of the problem. Meeting on 6 January, 1989, Homa and Simonson had also concluded that any hope of reaching the target of 100 per cent return required swift action, getting the message out and more careful tracking of where the coffeemakers were in the recall reverse distribution system. They felt a more comprehensive strategy would also help protect Black & Decker's reputation and assist in convincing customers to wait for a replacement unit.

Simonson was put in charge of the recall. For the next six months it was her team's number one priority. Proposals for a communications campaign had been immediately solicited from two of HPG's external agencies: the New York advertising agency McCann-Erickson and the New York public relations firm Geltzer and Company. On 9 January, both organisations presented their ideas.

McCann-Erickson suggested three advertising scenarios:

- A one-time national notification plan, such as a half-page advertisement in *Newsweek*, or 40 30-second spots on national radio for one week.
- A one-month, high-coverage, high-awareness campaign including extensive advertising in national magazines and four weeks of commercials on ten radio networks, an effort that would reach 85 to 90 per cent of adults.
- A two-week, intermediate-level campaign, working in tandem with publicity that, with advertising similar to that suggested in the second approach but over a shorter time period, would reach about 77 per cent of adults.

The costs of these alternative ranged from $39,000 to $950,000. Simonson encouraged McCann-Erickson to develop the creative work for its proposals, though she intended to await the outcome of the initial publicity programme before turning to advertising.

Geltzer proposed establishing an HPG/agency task force to handle the public relations programme. This would be designed to persuade consumers to replace the faulty coffeemakers while emphasising that the recall was voluntary and reinforcing the profile of Black & Decker as a responsible corporation committed to quality. A revised press release would be prepared, including photographs of the coffeemaker, background on Black & Decker's record of excellence, safety and service, and an attention-getting label identifying the material as 'an urgent message from Black & Decker'. The press kits would be followed up by telephone calls. There would also be a consumer affairs media blitz, point-of-purchase materials, the distribution of public service announcement radio tapes, a recall liaison at the January housewares trade show, trade press materials and special information for employees and stockholders. The taskforce would review progress and report to senior management weekly as well as compiling and maintaining a recall manual. Geltzer estimated the cost would be about $90,000.

Take two

After evaluating the alternatives, Simonson and her team – with Heiner's support – decided to implement the Geltzer strategy in combination with an intensive direct marketing approach. This latter tactic required a sophisticated database to track consumers and returns, a project that was handled by HPG's information systems group. Ultimately more than 70,000 names of likely owners were included on the list, from sources as diverse as owner registration records for other Spacemaker products to contestants who entered a competition in *Good Housekeeping* that had the coffeemaker as a prize. Callers to the recall freephone were also added to the database and each person on the list was sent a letter, a recall checklist and a reply card. On this last document, respondents were to indicate:

- Never owned product
- Yes! I own and will return
- Yes! Returned product (specifying where)
- Refuse to return product.

Those that did not answer were sent follow-up notices. Registered post was used for much of the correspondence to ensure receipt and protect against product liability litigation. Certain highly probable owners were even contacted by telephone. In addition, to reach the trade, a similarly detailed mailing went out to the store managers of every outlet stocking the coffeemaker, and the exact location of units was noted as precisely as possible. This database recall system is shown in Figure 8.1 and Table 8.1.

Table 8.1 Plan to close consumers

	Known owners	High probability owners	Low probability owners
First approach – mail package	Recorded post	Recorded post	First-class post
Second approach to 'no replies' after 10 days	Phone	Recorded post parcel	First-class post parcel
Third approach to 'no replies' after 10 days	Phone or closure letter depending on earlier conversation	Phone	Post parcel

Complementing this work, Geltzer's public relations campaign was initiated with a new press release on 11 January, 1989. The free substitute coffeemaker along with the Spacemaker Plus replacement or a refund were emphasised. Heiner was also quoted commenting on the potential

Database-driven Recall System

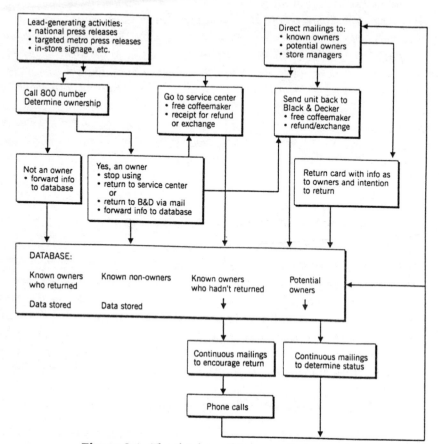

Figure 8.1 The database-driven recall system

danger of the existing coffeemaker and stating that the recall only had consumers' 'best interests in mind'. Supported with an extensive telephone follow-up, this strategy was quite successful. Within two days the recall was mentioned on 22 television stations, 52 radio stations and in a number of large-circulation newspapers. Calls to the freephone increased significantly.

Reinforcing the recall message, photos of the coffeemaker and a Black & Decker representative were released over the wire services; public service announcements were distributed to 3,000 smaller radio stations and 355 television stations; consumer talk show radio tapes were mailed; and an article on the recall was written and sent to 3,800 smaller daily and weekly papers. To stimulate returns from retail outlets, a reminder mailing went out to store managers; telephone calls were made; and salespeople were asked to remind 'tardy accounts'. Discreet signs were printed with a tear-off information sheet for display in retail stores.

Reviewing progress at the end of January 1989, the recall team's records showed that 48,462 of the 53,400 coffeemakers estimated to be in the hands of the trade and 7,760 of the 35,000 units estimated to be owned by consumers had been returned, a 64 per cent overall return rate. Still to come, Simonson and her team planned another mailing and telephone follow-up to likely owners, one that would tactfully increase pressure on those who had or were thought very likely to have one of the recalled coffeemakers. A third press release was issued on 31 January.

TYING UP LOOSE ENDS

In early February, new information indicated that the number of coffeemakers estimated to have been sold to individuals should be reduced from 35,000 to nearer 25,000 units. Based on this and continuing returns, by 7 February, more than 74,000 (approximately 84 per cent) of the defective products had been located and/or returned, including over 17,000 units with consumers. This meant that about 14,000 units had not been traced. To persuade the remaining consumers to participate in the recall, Simonson and her team again considered an advertising campaign, but soon decided that a 'poor performers' direct marketing and public relations programme would do the job.

This most focused component of the recall programme was begun in early March and targeted geographic groups of consumers who had notably low response rates. Of the 80 largest cities in the United States, 24 were categorised as 'underachievers', and special press releases were prepared comparing, for instance, the less than 20 per cent return rate of Philadelphia to the nearly 76 per cent rate of Chicago. The Milwaukee release, for example, was headed: 'Milwaukeeans Slow to Return Recalled Products'.

There were also retail outlets that still had stock, and one was even discovered continuing to display the coffeemaker three months after the recall announcement. Salespeople became the primary means of pressuring these merchants, with HPG suggesting it would not supply the relaunched coffeemaker to stores that failed to return faulty units. Consumer delays in returning the recalled product, once they were made aware of the recall, were in large measure due to a desire to keep the coffeemaker or an underestimate of the risk this involved. The failure of retailers to comply, however, largely reflected their operational inefficiencies.

After evaluating progress, Simonson and her team felt that, with a likely 85 per cent ultimate rate, 1 June, 1989 should be the deadline for individuals to receive a free replacement coffeemaker. By the end of May, Black & Decker had received 82 per cent of the Spacemaker Plus units. By 1 November, it had 87 per cent of the distributed stock: 50,738 from dealers and 25,850 from consumers. At this point, HPG management concluded that the remaining units were with people who could not be reached or who did not wish to comply.

In December, a survey of 512 consumers involved in the recall found that 70 per cent were 'very satisfied' and 94 per cent 'very or somewhat satisfied' with the recall. This was in spite of the delay of the replacement coffeemaker from May until October 1989. According to forms returned to service centres, consumers claimed to have learned about the recall in the following ways:

Letter	30%
Newspaper	25%
Radio	9%
TV	12%
Other	24%

Despite the substantial direct and indirect costs of the recall, Black & Decker was convinced its actions created goodwill and possibly saved lives. As one customer wrote:

> The gesture of providing a free older-model coffeemaker, plus the refund, plus the added effort of send the cheque via Airborne Express, displays an unusual and very refreshing sense of corporate responsibility on the part of Black & Decker.
>
> Our friends and acquaintances are already hearing about the above-and-beyond-the-call-of-duty response of your company.

Black & Decker attributes the success of the recall to:

- The ease of product identification
- The targeting of each unit in the field through direct marketing
- Providing a compelling incentive to return the product, including the free, less expensive coffeemaker and the replacement machine when available or a full refund (take-up on the refund was surprisingly low)
- Openness and honesty in communications
- Turnkey logistics for consumers and channels
- Perhaps most important, taking the recall seriously.

At the end of 1989, Black & Decker had achieved an unprecedented 92 per cent return rate.

Acknowledgement

This chapter is based on Smith Craig N (1990), 'Black & Decker Corporation: Spacemaker Plus Coffeemaker (A) and (B)', Harvard Business School Publishing, Boston, Case number 9-590-099 and 9-590-100.

Note

1. Spacemaker Plus is trademark of the General Electric Company, USA.

9

APPLYING RESEARCH TO DECISION MAKING*

Stephen King

OUTLINE

This chapter is the text of a speech given to the annual conference of the Market Research Society in 1983. It was lighthearted in tone, but its thesis was very serious. It was that market research was often being so badly misused that it was actually harming the process of marketing innovation. Since then the economic pressures on companies have greatly intensified, and this means that the dangers outlined have become greater. The text may be more valid today than when it was first written.

In the past, companies often failed through taking the public for granted or misinterpreting people's knowledge, needs and desires. It was the marketing revolution and its use of market research that put the consumer at the heart of the commercial process.

But today companies have grown in size and bureaucracy, and under competitive pressures marketing people have started to play by the rules and look for safety. Many of them almost expect market research to tell them what to do. They value it by how much its results can be applied directly to decision making. The pendulum may have swung too far.

The weakness of post-war British marketing has been in innovation: that is, a failure to provide a constant stream of product and service improvements. Market research has played a part in this failure: not through its skills and techniques, but through the way in which its results have been used. Much of the misuse has come from a mistaken belief that there is little value in it unless its findings can be applied directly and immediately to marketing decisions.

By contrast, there is enormous value in research, provided it is seen as an aid to and an essential part of the process of innovation. This chapter puts forward a simplified model of how innovation actually happens. It

---

* This chapter first appeared in *Marketing Intelligence and Planning*, 1, 3, 1983, and also in *MRS Newsletter*, 208, June 1983, pp 28–33.

implies three distinct roles for consumer research, none of which is that of acting as a substitute for managerial judgement. The three roles are;

- To build up background understanding and illuminate the problem to be solved
- to stimulate ideas
- to evaluate the experiments that arise from those ideas.

Today's companies will not survive without innovation, and they will find it difficult to innovate without using consumer research properly.

INTRODUCTION

Marketing and market research have been two of the great post-war growth industries. Their *achievement* over the last 30 years has been a touch less impressive. Figure 9.1 shows the UK's share of world trade and import penetration in manufactured goods. You can see that in 30 years our share of world trade declined from 26 per cent to 9.5 per cent, while import penetration grew from 5 per cent to 26 per cent. Whatever the precise balance of the many underlying causes, there can be no doubt that this is the *mechanism* of relative economic decline – a substantial loss of market share, both at home and abroad.

Of course, there has been a very great deal of excellent market research in the UK – it is probably better than in any other country. But I'm very

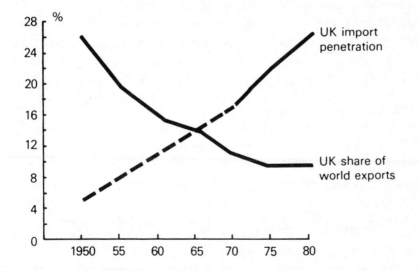

Source: Department of Trade

Figure 9.1 UK trade in manufactured goods 1950–80

much less happy about the way in which a lot of it is *used*. In fact, I think there has been some use of research which has actually contributed to the unhappy direction of the lines on the chart. If I'm right, we'd better see what, as the Market Research Society, we can do about it.

So what does lie behind this mechanism of relative decline? Let's take just one specific example: textile machinery. This was a market that the UK dominated in the late nineteenth century, with some 80 per cent of world trade and virtually no import penetration. By 1955, the world market had greatly expanded, but we still had 30 per cent of it. However, in the next 20 years, the UK share dropped to 11 per cent. Germany took up most of it, becoming the world market leader, with Switzerland and Japan getting the rest.

At the same time as our exports weakened, the UK started importing textile machinery. Between 1970 and 1975, 89 per cent of textile manufacturers bought foreign machines, and the average price of those machines was about 20 per cent higher than the machines that we exported. A survey was mounted to see why they'd done so (Rothwell 1980). Of the reasons given 45 per cent were that the foreign machines worked better, were more advanced designs. Thirty-eight per cent were that there simply wasn't a suitable UK machine available (and that tended to be suitability in terms of quality, modernity and standards). Nine per cent were that the foreign firms seemed to understand the user better and gave better service. Only 4 per cent were on the grounds of price.

It seemed very clear, with all the other findings in the survey, that the basic UK problem was a *lack of innovation*. By innovation I do not mean the grand, one-off, fundamental, breakthrough invention. I do not mean a process like the discovery of the structure of DNA or the invention of the jet engine. When I talk about innovation here, I mean a constant stream of minor improvements, modifications, regular small advances in design, in quality, in service or in utility.

It seems to me that behind the decline over the last 30 years in British textile machinery lies a failure to develop this sort of stream of improvement. As NEDO put it: 'The long-term fall in the UK export share appears to be associated with a fall in the relative quality or sophistication of UK exports, ie their non-price competitiveness rather than a decline in their price competitiveness.' And there are many UK markets where imports seem to have led in innovation – for instance cars, motorbikes, tyres, electronic goods and some domestic durables.

Or take packaged grocery brands. An excellent analysis by John Madell (1980) of BMP looked at the fate of new brands. Of 585 new food brands he identified as being launched and advertised between 1969 and 1976,

53 per cent were dead, off the market, by 1978. Forty-three per cent were still alive, but selling at under £4 million at retail selling price. Only 4 per cent, 21 brands from the original 585, were selling more than £4 million a year.

In many ways, I think the 43 per cent walking wounded will often have been more destructive to their companies than the outright failures, because over a long period they will have been taking up time, resources and commitment which would have given a far better return if applied to innovation and improvement of the old established brands at the centre of the company's business.

Now the fundamental reasons why new brands so often fail are really quite clear. There have been many analyses and they all come essentially to the same conclusion. One of the most vivid was Hugh Davidson's (1976). He took 50 successful new brands and 50 failures, and looked at various aspects of them to work out why. Briefly, he showed that price was not critical; the failures tended to be more expensive than competitors, but so were the successes. But performance, as measured by blind product tests, was crucial; three-quarters of the brands with a better performance than the competition succeeded, three-quarters of those with the same performance or worse failed. Exactly the same with distinctiveness. Seventy per cent of those that were not very different from competitors failed, 70 per cent of those that were very different succeeded.

In other words, all the analyses suggest that to succeed in packaged goods, the new brand has to be 'better and different'. So innovation is absolutely critical here too. What is disturbing is that, from the very terms in which Hugh Davidson did his analysis, the 50 failures had their blind product tests just as the successes did. Presumably many of the results were in some way misused.

FLAGSHIP BRANDS

If new brands all too often fail for lack of innovation, what about the old-established brands? A few years ago I did an analysis of 67 'flagship' brands (King 1980). These were food brands, and they were all the food brands that were on the market from 1964 to 1978 and also spent at least £250,000 on press and TV advertising in 1977. That is, the old-established brands central to their companies' success. What was most fascinating was their pricing history. Over the 14-year period 1964–78, the retail price index for food went up 308 per cent; but the flagship brands went up in price by only 211 per cent. To put it another way, if their prices had kept up with those for food in general, they would have been selling in 1978 at 30 per cent more than they actually were.

That is a huge gap, and I am fairly sure that it can only be explained by concluding that, in face of huge pressure from retailers, intense competition from other manufacturers and high inflation in raw materials, on the whole these manufacturers took the negative approach. They underestimated the consumer's growing desire for quality and they cut back on everything to do with future progress – research and development, process improvement, product improvement, packaging, advertising and market research. Meanwhile, private label brands tended to improve in quality. In the end, many manufacturer brands didn't get higher prices because they didn't deserve them (Bennett and Cooper 1981). Manufacturing companies got into a vicious spiral – the 'crisis in branding' which has been a topic of such anguish for marketing people for the last decade or so (King 1978).

Again, the crisis in branding seems to me in essence a problem of innovation at the product level – a failure to introduce a constant stream of improvements in order to keep ahead of competitors and private label and to satisfy social change. Yet all these flagship brands must surely have had market research available. Did they have the wrong sort of research? Or did they use it wrongly? Or did they ignore it?

Clearly one can't generalise, but I do think there is some evidence that a lot of market research is wrongly used; and I believe that the misuse is very much related to the theme of this conference – 'The application of market research to decision making'.

I came across two pieces of evidence recently put to the MRS (Market Research Society) about what marketing people are looking for in market research. First, Michael Leach (1980), a real live marketing person, said: 'Marketing people do not have the time, probably not the willingness and maybe not even the expertise to decipher the important [in research] from the unimportant. So the requirement for the researchers to lead the marketing person by the hand is crucial'. I think that what he was really saying was: 'Look, fellows, cut out the fancy stuff. Give me market research results that I can apply *directly* to my day-to-day concerns, especially the guerrilla war against the retailers'. In Professor Dahrendorf's terms, he was interested in questions rather than problems (Dahrendorf 1983).

Rather more explicit evidence from Martin Simmons (1982) showed that marketing managers thought market research agencies to be fairly reliable, with quite good standards and a good understanding of the marketing process. But there was an appreciable desire among marketing managers for market researchers to 'get off the fence and recommend courses of action'. They were saying in effect: 'It's not enough to tell me what's going on; tell me what to do about it. Let's have some research that is *action orientated.*' They wanted research that could be *directly applied* to decision making (I suppose rather as you apply paint to a wall). What I'd like to do now is consider some of the implications of this sort of approach, and what it's done for the use of market research.

Let's start with the most action-orientated, decision-making-orientated research – the retail audit. Maybe some of you don't sit in on retail audit presentations, so let me explain how they go. There's a meeting of the top people in the company, all neatly sorted out into hierarchies. The managing director sits in the front row. Not only can he see the figures on the chart, he can see the presenter's crib of pencilled comments on them. Suddenly he turns round to the deputy sales manager, North East, and says: 'Carruthers, 20 per cent out of stock in Tyne Tees'. Carruthers, who sits a long way back and can't read the figures but knew that something like this was going to come up one day, says the first thing that comes into his head, which is: 'We've got a 15 for 12 discount coming up and a tailor-made overrider and a new consignment of shelf-wobblers'. The managing director, who doesn't know what any of that means, says 'Well, make sure that you do', and puts a tick in his Action this Day Noddy pocketbook and feels that the whole thing has been worthwhile.

Actually, what the research says is that on the day of the audit, and that day only, some six weeks ago, if you're lucky, about 20 per cent of shops were out of stock, give or take a few either way. The action called for could be something completely different. For instance, if the brand involved was a seasonal alcoholic drink, the proper action might be to organise a really good 24-hour emergency delivery service next Christmas – not 'get moving on it, Carruthers, today'. I think that the greatest value in retail audit research lies in the understanding it can give of long-term cause and effect. But it tends to be treated as a here-and-now, action-orientated description of what happened yesterday, because the terms in which it is reported are those of the daily preoccupations of marketing people – retailers, prices, stocks, deliveries and out-of-stock.

Let's take another of the big spenders – the TV ratings from the well-loved BARB (Broadcaster's Audience Research Board). This research again is concerned with questions in the Dahrendorfian sense – the marketing person's question: 'What am I getting for my TV spending then?' Let's say the company has been fortunate enough to get a 20-rating spot among housewives in the London area. In reporting this, the agency media person should say something along the lines of: 'Well, bearing in mind the panel size, at the 95 per cent confidence level you had a cost per thousand housewives of somewhere between about £8 and about £12'. He would then go on to add: 'I am, of course, ignoring the very considerable problem of attention values, the current difficulties of measuring the use of videotape recorders and watching on second sets. I'm assuming, as we always do, that people are perfectly able accurately to assess that they have watched at least eight minutes out of fifteen and that zapping between channels is randomly distributed. We must, of course, remind ourselves too that we won't ever get this precise pattern of competitive programmes again, to guide us about future ratings for a similar spot'. He could drone on for several more minutes on the limitations of the data and the uncertainty of their meaning.

The agency media person doesn't, of course, say any of this. He presents, without comment, a densely packed page of computer printout. A vast entrail-gazing industry has sprung up, in TV companies and advertising agencies and marketing companies and research companies, dedicated to taking informed guesses to four places of decimals – in the name of action-orientation.

Let's take another important problem that has been turned into a question: 'What motivates people to buy my brands?' For centuries philosophers, psychologists, biologists and all sorts of academics have puzzled about what goes on in the human mind. They have reached no sort of common conclusion. Rather little of this academic work has filtered through to the world of marketing, probably because it's not sufficiently action-orientated. Perhaps the best bridge comes from anthropologists. Mary Douglas (1982), in particular, has written about why people buy goods, saying 'goods are for thinking with'. In a splendid piece called 'Beans Mean Thinks' (1977) she wrote: 'consumption decisions are a vital source of the *culture* of the time. . . The individual uses consumption to *say something* about himself and his family and his locality'.

Despite this sort of insight and the complexity of academics' views about what goes on in the mind, marketing people are looking for simple answers about the motivations for buying their brands, because they want market research to tell them what to do. They're hoping for a nice, neat, rank-ordered list of motivations so that the top half-dozen can be stuffed directly into products and advertising. There are various sorts of research that have pandered to this demand, and I think that all of them tend to treat the mind as if it were some sort of mixed box of Lego waiting to be put together.

For instance, put yourself into the frame of mind of a real consumer, a respondent, a person. I tried to think of something for which everyone in this audience is sometimes in the market, and picked on houses. So, imagine you're thinking of buying a house and this nice lady interviewer comes along. She asks: 'Which of these features of a house is most important to you – walls, doors, windows, heating, roof, being 345 yards form a tube station open until 11.43 pm, green front door, mock half-timbers, attractive garden, no dry rot. . .?' And it goes on for another three pages, because of course today the computer can cope with the answers; indeed, to be economic, it needs to be regularly and fully fed.

TRADE-OFF

Maybe there is less of this particular type of action-orientated research going on today than there used to be, but there's a sort of Son of Primitive Compartmentalism coming along in some of today's refinements. Take trade-off research, for instance. That can give us questions like: 'Q.346c. Would you rather have a house with a roof, heating and a green front door *or* a house with walls, windows and a lean-to conservatory? Q.346d. Would you rather have a house with two recep, an attractive garden and one of those bells that go "ding-dong" *or* a house with a roof, a wealth of oak beams and a lock-up garage?' Plus 108 more combinations, because the computer wants to show it can deal with them.

Or we can move on to the Fishbein version of the Lego of the mind, with questions like – 'On the whole, would you say that your mother would approve or disapprove of your buying a house with leaded lights?' – all on a lovely seven-point scale. And the answers can be carefully multiplied by other data to be fed directly into decision making.

Another rich area for the mechanistic application of research is econometrics. Let me give you a quick example. Figure 9.2 represents what an organisation called the Yellow Fats Marketing Council might be looking at to try to explain the rather unfavourable trends in butter consumption. They ask why butter sales are down and set out to model the market. The figures shown here are all quite genuine, but for the sake of simplicity I've used only two independent variables in the model.

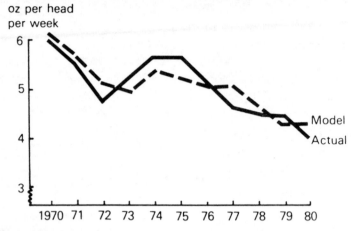

Source: NFS, CSO, IBM Statpack

Figure 9.2 Butter consumption: actual versus model

You can see that the model gives a fairly good fit. In fact, I know it was a good fit because the computer used for the regression analysis told me that the multiple correlation was 0.90338. (It must be accurate because there are five place of decimals.) The R squared adjusted is 0.77013, which isn't bad, and the F value is a massive 17.51.

In other words, this simple model with just two variables can clearly be applied directly to decision making. Because all this is published data, and you can do the exercise for yourselves, I can reveal what the equation was. It was:

$$B = 8.59225 - 0.00089V - 0.00080M$$

where:

   B = butter consumption (oz per head per week)
   V = business visits abroad ('000 per year)
   M = consumer spending on motor vehicles (£ million at 1975 prices).

This is clearly action-orientated. The government must be the prime target group and the YFMC must clearly be pressing them to bring back exchange controls on businesspeople and bring back hire purchase controls on cars or put up the car tax. I think you can see from the 1983 Budget that part of this strategy seems to have worked.

Of course, every one of us here has piously pointed out at times that correlation isn't causation; but I'm not sure we always take it into account in our hidden assumptions. I don't think anybody should ever use the term 'best fit' without a blush and without rereading Andrew Ehrenberg's elegant piece 'How Good is Best?' (1982).

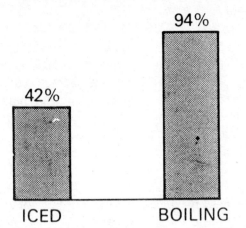

Figure 9.3 Gap analysis: per cent who like tea

Another very fertile field for mechanistic decision making via research is new product development. Many of the systems are designed as filters or ways of preventing things happening, but there are some which purport to be directly applicable to inventing new products (Holmes and Keegan 1983). Figure 9.3 symbolises the use of gap analysis, for instance.

These simple figures would be used to demonstrate that since a lot of people like iced tea and a lot like boiling tea, there is an immense potential market for warm tea. The reason for this is that between the two columns, though sadly it can't be picked out by the naked eye, is a very large amount of *n*-dimensional concept space. And within that *n*-dimensional concept space there are masses of new products just waiting to be analysed into the open. This is just one of many infallible systems based on the idea that you can invent by deduction. Somehow an invention can be produced by a step-by-step method, untouched by human mind.

This deductive approach is by no means confined to quantitative research. All over the London suburbs are little collections of eight shoppers who are expected to tell manufacturers what the strategies and brand positioning for new brands should be. They are there to pass judgement on and discriminate between things called Concepts – a sort of Platonic idea of a brand from which all emotion has been drained. Once these modern Delphic oracles have chosen the ideal concept, the manufacturer can of course hype it up with the optional extras like naming, advertising and packaging, and sprinkle a little brand image over the whole dish.

ADVERTISING RESEARCH

Perhaps the most overt attempt to apply research directly to decision making has been in off-the-peg advertising research. Advertising research is an unusual type in that as often as not the research method is chosen first and the problem to be solved is only sorted out afterwards, if indeed at all. This happens because it's terribly hard to know how advertising works. So people say: 'At least let's pick a measure that we know how to use'. It's as if an art critic said 'I don't know how to measure artistic merit, but I do understand how this tape measure works, so we'll use that'.

The trouble is that any measure used implies some model of how advertising works; there is no way of evading the problem. Lurking behind most off-the-peg advertising research systems are some very questionable ideas; for instance that the mind is some sort of inert and passive receptacle for messages, an intellectual sponge, or that all advertising works by converting people *in toto* from Brand A to Brand B. Or that it always works by rational persuasion. What nearly all the off-the-peg systems have in common is that their underlying models are opposed to more or less every other theory there has ever been about how the mind works or how markets behave. They're based on our trying to measure what ads do to people rather than starting at the other end and asking what people do with ads, how they use them and how they respond to them. Once again, I think, the desire for action-orientation tends to push us into misuse of research.

There's a marked contrast to this in the case histories put forward for the Institute of Practitioners in Advertising (IPA) Advertising Effectiveness Awards. The winners, presented in *Advertising Works* and now *Advertising Works 2* (Broadbent 1981, 1983), show how market research is used at its best. I don't think a single entry relied on just one measure of how advertising worked. What the judges were looking for, and what they found, was a *convincing argument* based on the interpretation of many different forms of research.

I think that these case histories symbolise how we should use all these forms of research that I have been commenting on. Just to make it absolutely clear, I am very much in favour of most of them *as research methods*. I couldn't live happily without retail audits and consumer panels. I do find valuable insights in the concept of trade-off. I've found Fishbein's work very fruitful when I try to understand people's motivations. I am a great believer in, and advocate of, the use of econometrics and market modelling. I'm greatly stimulated by both quantitative and qualitative research. But I also think that each of these can be, and quite often has been, destructive to innovation, and that, where this happens, it tends to be because of a desire to apply them *directly* to decision making.

In other words, I believe that part of our national failure to innovate has come through trying to use market research not as an *aid* to innovators, but as a *system* that ideally reduces all personal judgement to a decision as to which of two numbers is the larger. In my view, there are two main reasons for this. First, I believe that too many marketing people have clung to the wrong model of the process of innovation, and, second, I think that all too often we have the wrong sort of organisation for innovation. Let me take each of these in turn.

INNOVATION

The process

Choosing the right model of the innovation process seems to me to relate to a choice between two schools of science. (This is obviously a very simple analysis, since there are clearly many variants in schools of science, but I still think the distinctions made here are valid.) The old science, Baconian science, was essentially a four-stage process. You start off with controlled observation. Second, you accumulate data. Third, some sort of general laws emerge. Fourth, you verify these general laws with more observations and that becomes new knowledge – a sort of brick-by-brick progress. Then you can apply the new knowledge to specific instances. It's a sort of playing-safe science, with no shots in the dark. It seems to me that this is the sort of science that lies behind what I've been describing as misuse of market research – that is, the attempt to discover general laws which can be applied directly to decision making.

What I think of as the new science evolved gradually, following challenges to Newton's theories, and has been described most vividly by Karl Popper (1959) and his disciples. (I hesitate to mention Popper, because I think there has been great competition in the MRS to be Popperer than thou and argue on matters of textual criticism – see Alt and Brighton 1981; Lawrence 1982. What I will be referring to here is much more concerned with what I believe to be the spirit rather than the letter of Popper.) The key difference in the new science, I believe, was put by Popper as: 'Observations are always interpretations of the facts observed. They are interpretations in the light of theories '. Or, as Einstein put it: 'Theory cannot be fabricated out of the results of observation. It can only be invented'.

In other words, you can't make any sense out of the facts until you've had an idea. Whereas in the old science there's a step-by-step, risk-free build-up of knowledge which can then be directly applied, the new science involves inventing a trial solution right from the very beginning.

Very loosely based on these ideas, I'd like to put forward what seems to me the proper process of innovation – a five-stage process – as it applies to marketing, summarised in Figure 9.4.

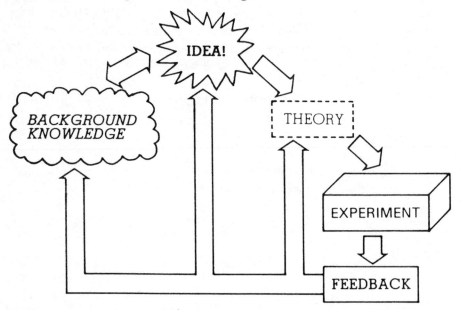

Figure 9.4 How innovation happens

First, we have to have some background knowledge, an *understanding* of the people and issues and the motivations in the market. That includes some understanding of what is the right problem to solve, what is the situation that we want to improve.

Second, we have to have an idea. In Popper's language, we could call it the vision of a trial solution, often to a trial problem. The idea clearly relates to the background knowledge, but doesn't emerge directly, deductively and logically from it. Everyone who has written about having ideas has made the point that it is a non-logical process; it is essentially subconscious and is often extremely messy. All the devices that are available to stimulate ideas – like brainstorming and synectics and Edward de Bono's lateral thinking – are in essence deliberate interruptions to the normal logical flow. Or as James Webb Young (1972) wrote: 'At this stage what you have to do is drop the subject. . . Out of nowhere the idea will come; it will come to you when you are least expecting it'.

Thirdly, the idea has to be patted into shape; some sort of coherent theory has to be put forward – a hypothesis, a sentence which starts with 'I wonder if. . .'. The implications of this theory have to be put into some form that is testable: in our case, usually something physical. This is a stage in which marketing tends to differ from 'real science'. Very often in scientific tests there are just two alternatives to be tested against each other. In marketing there is an enormous amount of judgement involved in putting the theory into physical form, since there is a huge variety of forms into which it might be put.

Fourth, there is an experiment. I use the word here in its popular sense – not a scientifically controlled experiment, but a 'let's give it a whirl and see what happens' type of experiment. I doubt if there could ever be such a thing as a true scientifically controlled experiment in marketing. Our competitors, like fish, simply won't sit still to be counted. At our nearest approach to real science, there tend to be irreducible placebo effects. I think the real contribution that Popper made at this stage was in effect to say that what we should attempt to do is not verify, but try to disprove. In the terms of our own less rigorous experiments, what one has to do is challenge the theory, and that can be a constructive and exciting process. As Popper put it: 'It is part of the greatness and the beauty of science that we can learn, through our own critical investigation, that the world is utterly different from what we ever imagined'.

The fifth stage is of course feedback of the results of the experiment. This can help at three different stages of the next cycle. It adds to our background knowledge, and indeed can modify our statement of the problem. (We often don't really understand a problem fully until we've tried to solve it.) It can directly stimulate a new idea. And it can modify or improve our theory.

This is all clearly a continuous cyclical process. In marketing we are constantly trying to learn and improve, not to discover some final solution. What this five-stage theory of the process of innovation does is make much clearer what the roles for market research are. There seem to me to be three main roles:

- First, research can help at stage one in giving people understanding, building up the background knowledge, illuminating the problem to be solved or the situation to be improved and interpreting the flow of past solutions. And I think there is a strong case in marketing, as elsewhere, for doing a certain amount of 'beautiful research' – research into an area which might, or might not, turn out to be interesting, even if no one can think in advance how they might want to use the results. We will never be in a position to exploit the unexpected, if we insist on measuring only the near-certain.

- The second role for research is at stage two – to stimulate ideas directly. This is typically what much small-scale qualitative research had been used for. It seems to me that if we don't make it clear that this is a specific and important role, we will go on having those dreary arguments in which one lot of people say 'qualitative research isn't really respectable' and another lot say 'we find qualitative research particularly valuable'. At the same time, I can't for the life of me understand why advocates of quantitative research don't make more of the stimulus to ideas which it can undoubtedly offer.
- The third role is, of course, at stage five – measuring what's happened when you've tried out an experiment.

Where I think there isn't really a role for research within this innovation process is decision making. That is, I cannot see any scope for its *direct* application to decision making. Its values are enormous throughout the process, but they are essentially indirect. Even when we are at the challenging experiments stage – let's say a product test – we are still only discriminating between a few testable forms of our theory. We can say from research whether, in the terms of the test dimensions, A, B or C performs better. But we can't say whether there may, or may not, be many other testable forms of this or another theory that would perform massively better.

So what I am saying is that the first important reason for misuse of research is a tendency to cling to the old, wrong model of the innovation process, and so to the wrong roles for research. And the second lies, I think, in the way in which some companies organise themselves.

The organisation

If you consider the sort of organisation that is best for real invention, you'll usually conclude that it's essentially a purposive project group. It will need a fair amount of institutionalised 'straddling'. If, for instance, you are trying to develop a radically new brand, there will be constant trial and feedback; all the elements of the new brand will interact – the formula interacts with the taste and the taste interacts with the colour and the colour interacts with the packaging and the packaging interacts with the advertising and the advertising interacts with the formula. The production line approach of A doing his bit and handing it to B who does his bit and hands it over to C, etc simply won't work. There has to be a project group and a group leader and an interacting team of specialists.

If we are dealing with innovation as I've defined it – the constant stream of minor improvement, that is rather less demanding than real invention. But it seems to me that we still need most of the same elements of organisation, for the same reasons.

But what we find in most marketing companies is something very different from project groups. We find a full-scale traditional family-tree type organisation with clearly defined hierarchies, functionally separate departments and strongly entrenched departmental barriers. Now that might be fine for building up and improving efficient routines (which is of course very necessary in companies) but it's pretty hopeless for innovation. All too often any sort of communication between departments is difficult and formalised, let alone that sort of informal iconoclastic project work that I've been describing and the essential messiness of idea generation. It's all too easy to see why, in the hierarchical sort of organisation, there is a call for the direct application of research to decision making.

Martin Christopher and Gordon Wills once said: 'The key participants in the marketing decision-making arena are the accountant and the manufacturing director' (Christopher and Wills 1982). I think that's a rather stark way of putting it, but I see what they mean. I think I would put it more like this: if we want a real brand management, proper decision making about marketing, we have to have a project group working at the top – say, a group consisting of managing director, manufacturing director and marketing director. Only if such an authorative group works on a regular and interactive basis will a company have much chance of being good at innovation.

Even if this happens, there's another block to the sensible use of research. Think of the line of communication between the respondents and this top project group. First, you have real people out there answering questions. Then a market research agency, normally split between interviewer and analyst, who may sometimes talk to each other but usually not much. Then there is often some form of black box – a manipulation of the raw figures, in which the assumptions behind the maths may or may not be very clear. Then there is a report, in which the reworked figures are, very properly, selected and interpreted. Then, very often, you have the market research department in the company which has commissioned the research; and to justify its existence it may need further to reselect and reinterpret and summarise the report. (Sometimes it can do this inventively and practically; sometimes it acts as a form of heavy-handed bureaucratic purchasing officer.) The market research department may itself be regarded as a bunch of raving intellectuals who have little to do with real decision making. Either way, that's another barrier. There can be other filters too – such as brand managers and advertising agencies.

Finally, what the people said in answer to the questions will reach our top project group, the people who really manage innovation in the company. But after so long and hazardous a journey it would be surprising if the information were wholly fresh and ungarbled and if it were never misapplied.

CONCLUSIONS

There is a great deal of skilled and helpful market research in this country, and a great deal of successful marketing. But I think there is also evidence of weakness in innovation, and that this is fundamental to our relative economic decline. Part of the weakness, in my view, is a failure to understand the proper process of innovation, which leads to misuse of research. Market research is inevitably pulled into this by demand, and I think it is reasonable for us to consider, as members of the MRS, what we ought to be doing about it.

Clearly it is hard for individual researchers, as part of a service industry (and a cottage industry at that) to change the nature of the demand. But I do think we might consider where the MRS itself might concentrate its marketing strategy, its education and its evangelism. Here is a shortlist from me of areas for consideration.

Marketing

- Concentrate the MRS' own marketing activities much more on higher level management. Seek to influence not just the market research managers and marketing departments, but also managing directors, finance directors and manufacturing directors.
- Concentrate more on the roles for research and the uses for research, particularly within this innovation process – not just research techniques. That would include preaching the values of occasional beautiful research.

Organisation

- Make people aware of the values of the project group type of organisation in the innovative process.
- Advocate more firmly the values of long-term relationships between

research companies and their clients, especially in the growth of understanding that this brings, with the benefit of effectively shortening that communication chain.

- Bring out the problem of the long chain, and try to develop and market techniques that will bring the final users much closer to the original data or original respondents.
- Urge members to clarify some of their black boxes.

Experiments

Marketing people have no right to criticise market researchers for being too academic, if they themselves steadfastly refuse to mount marketing experiments. The MRS must press harder on this, perhaps sponsoring more education in the running and measurement of marketing experiments.

Role of the researcher

I think the MRS may have to take on the job of making it clearer what the role of the researcher is, since the individual may be in no position to do so.

It seems to me that researchers must be seen as experts on *what is*, not on *what to do about it*. Despite the demand for them to produce results that in effect take decisions, we should insist that their real role is to interpret and bring to life what goes on in the world. They cannot possibly know enough about all the other factors that lie behind decisions to be justified in advising marketing people what to do.

In fact, I think we should question very hard the whole idea of applying research directly to decision making. I hope that the next time the MRS has a conference on this sort of topic it will be called 'Research to stimulate innovation'.

REFERENCES

Alt M and Brighton M (1981), 'Analysing data or telling stories?', *JMRS*, Vol 24, No 4.

Bennett R C and Cooper R G (1981), 'The misuse of marketing', *Business Horizons*, Nov/Dec.

Broadbent S (ed) (1981), *Advertising Works*, IPA/Holt, Rinehart & Winston, London.

— (ed) (1983), *Advertising Works 2*, IPA/Holt, Rinehart & Winston, London.

Christopher M and Wills G (1982), 'Marketing research as action research', MRS Conference.

Dahrendorf R (1983), 'Research and decision making', *MRS Newsletter*, June.

Davidson J H (1976), 'Why most new consumer brands fail', *Harvard Business Review*, Vol 54, No 2,

Douglas M (1977), 'Beans means thinks', *The Listener*, 8 Sep.

— (1982), *In the Active Voice*, Routledge and Kegan Paul, London.

Ehrenberg A S C (1982), 'How good is best?', *Journal of the Royal Statistical Society*, Series A, 145, Part 3, pp 364–6.

Holmes C and Keegan S (1983), 'Current and Developing Creative Research Methods in New Product Development', MRS Conference.

King S H M (1978) *Crisis in Branding*, J Walter Thompson, London.

— (1980), *Advertising as a Barrier to Market Entry*, Advertising Association, London.

Lawrence R J (1982), 'To hypothesise or not to hypothesise?', *JMRS*, Vol 24, No 4.

Leach M L (1980), 'Marketing in the 80s – The Challenge for Research', MRS Conference.

Madell J (1980), 'New Products: How to Succeed When the Odds are Against You', *Marketing Week*, 22 Feb.

Popper K R (1959), *The Logic of Scientific Discovery*, Hutchinson, London.

Rothwell R (1980), 'Innovation in textile machinery', in Pavitt K (ed), *Technical Innovation and British Economic Performance*, Macmillan, London.

Simmons M (1982), 'The image of the British market research industry in the business world', MRS Conference.

Young J W (1972), *A Technique for Producing Ideas*, Crain Communications Inc, Chicago.

PART THREE

STRATEGIC ISSUES IN CONSUMER MARKETING

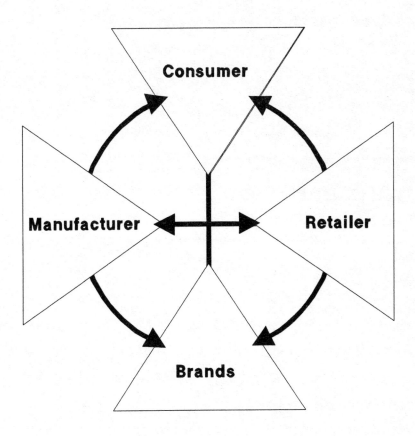

10

THE SERPENT IN THE SUPERMARKET'S PARADISE[*]

Keith Thompson

OUTLINE

As business becomes more and more international in character firms which were highly successful in the home market have wilted under increasing international competition. Consequently, Britain's balance of trade with the rest of the world continues to deteriorate. This chapter explores the relative failure of British firms in the international arena implicit in the long-term deterioration in the balance of trade by reference to one of the most successful industries of the last decade – food retailing.

It is sometimes claimed, not unreasonably, that British food retailers are the best in the world. Certainly, in terms of profitablity the major supermarket groups are in a world league of the their own. Yet, if service industries such as this are to fill the gap left by the depredation of manufacturers, they must be capable of making a positive contribution to Britain's external trade; and the major food retailers have not done that. Despite the growing internationalisation of the retail industry reinforced by the advent of a Single European Market, Britain's supermarket companies are voluntarily restricting themselves to the UK grocery market which accounts for a mere 10 per cent of the EC grocery market of which they are now a part.

Despite their world class credentials the supermarket groups remain insular compared with their more internationally minded European competitors. This chapter proposes that this parochialism by the otherwise competent and innovative supermarket directors is caused by structural inefficiences in the finance and corporate governance of British firms. Food retailers are the latest example of successful British enterprises that are unable to repeat their success when confronted by competitors which can rely upon a genuinely supportive business

---

[*] This chapter first appeared in *European Management Journal*, Vol. 10, No 1, Mar 1992.

environment. Clearly, as markets and businesses become increasingly global in character this has far-reaching implications for British industry.

'L'ANGLETERRE EST UNE NATION DE BOUTIQUIERS'

Bonaparte may well have been right, and Randlesome et al (1990) identify British shopkeepers as a major national strength, and probably the most efficient in Europe. So successful have British retailers been that it is said that they are a contributory factor in the UK's trade deficit, as through them importers have easy access to British markets (*The Sunday Times* 1990). By comparison, the limited horizons of foreign retailers protect their markets from international competitors; the inefficiencies of the Japanese distribution system amounting to a hidden form of protectionism.

The success of British supermarkets is in welcome contrast to the difficulties suffered by firms in the manufacturing industries where performance has continued to decline. As Doyle (1988) pointed out: the 'economic miracle' of the 1980s does not appear to have reversed a long-term trend, and gains in international competitiveness by British manufacturers have not led to export success. Over the last two decades Britain's share of world trade has halved, growth in manufacturing output was the lowest of all the advanced nations and Britain is the only industrial nation to have experienced an absolute decline in manufacturing output since 1973.

Unlike the manufacturers, Britain's major supermarket groups (Argyll, Asda, Sainsbury and Tesco) continued to make significant gains in market share and profitability throughout the 1980s. Bold innovative moves such as the implementation of centralised distribution and electronic point of sale (EPoS), product mix enhancements and increased superstore development helped them to gain market share whilst at the same time improving their margins to levels far beyond those of their international counterparts (Table 10.1). In many industries the simultaneous achievement of both these goals would be tantamount to defying gravity. Nevertheless, the supermarkets are hoping to repeat their success during the 1990s and are implementing massive capital expenditure programmes to that end (Salomon Bros 1991).

Given the declining balance of trade and the continuing problems of British manufacturers in world markets, it is encouraging to know that British supermarkets are world class competitors, well placed to take advantage of the Single European Market and the trend towards the globalisation of industries and markets.

Table 10.1	European grocery retailers: average net margin by country

	Average net margin (%)
UK	5–7
France	0.5–2.0
Holland	0.5–1.5
Belgium	0.5–1.5
Germany	0.5–1.5

Source: Banque Paribas (1989)

THE CHALLENGE OF EUROPE

The increasing internationalisation of retailing identified by for instance Hamill and Crosbie (1990), Treadgold (1989), Dawson et al (1988), Williams (1991) and others, is reinforced within Europe by the advent of the Single Market. Consequently, expansion-minded, internationally experienced European grocers are already building strong cross-border trading positions throughout the EC. Their targets include Britain, where the high margins available to food retailers are particularly attractive to competitors from other parts of Europe; Aldi (German) opened its first store in Britain in 1990 and plans to open a further 200 by 1993 (*Super Marketing* 1990). Dansk Supermarkd (Danish) is to open 30 'Netto' stores by the end of 1991, while GIB (Belgian), Carrefour (French), Tengelmann and Norma and Metro (German) are all said to be showing interest in the UK market (*The Grocer* 1990) (Figure 10.1).

British supermarkets are potentially strong international competitors. They are more concentrated and more profitable than their European counterparts who are particularly concerned to note that, compared to a similarly sized mainland European company, British retailers have twice to three times as much money available to spend on taking over a competitor (Delort 1990). Even so, none of the major British grocers have a presence in any other EC market. More surprisingly they apparently have no intention at all of competing in the wider EC market; Killen and Lees (1988), Thompson and Knox (1991), and Alexander (1989) all found that on the eve of the Single European Market none of the UK's major supermarket operators planned to enter any other European market. According to Nielsen (1990), British supermarkets are the most insular of any among the sixteen European countries which they surveyed. Asda and the Argyll Group have limited their participation in Europe to

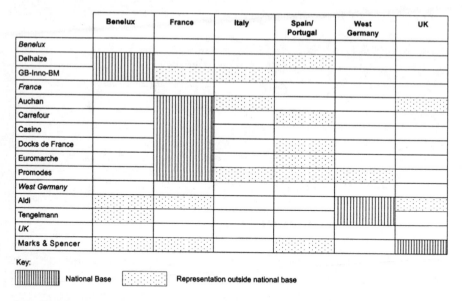

Key:

National Base ▓ | Representation outside national base ░

Source: Adapted from Debenham et al (1989).

Figure 10.1 European representation of selected EC grocery retailers

membership of buying groups and show no intention of extending their European presence to actually compete in mainland markets. Tesco chairman Sir Ian MacLaurin has said that it is unlikely that Tesco's expansion plans will include Europe, and that the company is more likely to enter the US market (*Super Marketing* 1991). Sainsbury has also decided to ignore Europe in favour of America. In the opinion of Ian Coull, Sainsbury's development director, 'North America with its Anglo-Saxon structure, presents a much more exciting opportunity' (than Europe) (*Retail Week* 1991).

British supermarket companies have shown themselves to be innovative, confident and willing to invest large amounts of money on new stores and new technology. Above all they have been successful in profitably expanding their businesses over many years. Now, faced with the opportunity of a Single European Market, they are failing to respond to the challenge. Far from grasping the opportunities offered by 1992, they are digging themselves in to defend the home market against more aggressive, internationally minded competitors. The danger for British food retailers is that those competitors will build a commanding lead in the most desirable European markets and effectively shut them out of what will be their 'home' market.

THE REASONS FOR RELUCTANCE TO COMPETE IN EUROPE

The main reasons advanced by the major supermarket groups for their reluctance to compete in Europe are:

1. Sufficient opportunities in Britain
2. Doubts about the exportability of food retailing
3. Lack of European market opportunities
4. Better opportunities in the US Market
5. The profit gap between the British and other EC retail food markets

These issues are addressed in the following sections.

Sufficient opportunities in Britain

Disregarding the prospect of complete diversification, Ansoff's tried-and-tested matrix offers the supermarkets three major intensive growth strategies; market penetration, product development and market development (Figure 10.2).

Market penetration

The salutory experience of price war in the 1960s led the major food retailing companies to concentrate on offering convenience, ease of parking and a wide range of choice as a means of 'desensitising'

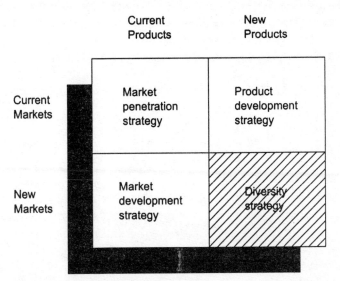

Source: Adapted from Ansoff (1957)

Figure 10.2 Ansoff's product/market expansion grid

consumers to price. It has been in the interest of the second division companies such as Gateway, Waitrose and Morrisons to go along with this. However, convenience, range and the perceived superiority of the major food retailers' brands has not been sufficient in recent years to increase market share at anything like the rate required by the current investment plans of the biggest supermarkets. As is common in maturing industries, each competitor appears to be planning for gains which are cumulatively well beyond the capacity of the market. Consumer expenditure on food grew at a compound rate of 0.4 per cent between 1985 and 1992 and is not expected to markedly improve during the rest of the 1990s. This is quite inadequate to sustain the ambitions of the biggest four food retailers. Industry analysts estimate that to achieve the targets implicit in their current investment plans the big four supermarkets will have to make market share gains of 5.2 per cent each year, an enormous task when compared with the annual gain of 1.6 per cent achieved in recent years. Such an aggressive market penetration strategy is likely to prompt a vigorous riposte from the intended victims – the middle ranking supermarket chains (Salomon Bros 1991).

Up until now the major supermarkets have managed to expand in a static market by taking business from small grocers and food shops (Table 10.2). However, the number of corner grocers is approaching an irreducible minimum, and the bigger supermarket operators' appetite for market share will soon force the second division supermarket companies to vigorously defend their share of the market. Since the main weapon at their disposal is to cut prices, the lasting effect of the market penetration strategies of the major supermarkets is likely to be a re-emergence of price-based competition and, consequently, lower margins.

Table 10.2   UK food sales by outlet size/type (%)

	1980	1982	1984	1986	1988	1990 (est)
Large grocers	40.8	46.5	51.3	55.1	59.4	64.2
Small grocers	18.2	16.1	12.6	11.4	10.3	9.8
Cooperattives	16.9	14.9	13.9	12.9	11.2	10.9
Others	24.9	22.5	22.2	20.6	19.0	15.1
Total	100.0	100.0	100.0	100.0	100.0	100.0

Source: Adapted from Euromonitor (1987), Mintel (1991)

Product development

In such an open and easily imitated industry as food retailing most of the radical product development gains have already been made and absorbed. The presence of fresh produce, wet fish, in-store bakeries, fresh meat, wine and beer now do no more than meet customer expectations.

Market development

The frontrunners are now moving beyond the simple addition of new food product lines and into newspapers, petrol, toiletries, cosmetics and (if allowed) prescription services. This is not a continuation of the practice of adding new products, it is a market development strategy which takes food retailers into new, non-food markets in which they have little expertise or competitive advantage. Petrol is a commodity sold on price rather than convenience, while newspaper sales require convenience of a sort not offered by supermarkets. Neither offers much opportunity to add value or, therefore, margin. Toiletries and cosmetics offer good margins but, as with petrol, newcomers to the market face stiff opposition from some very tough competitors like Boots and Superdrug or Shell and BP, for which these markets are life or death. Such markets do offer new opportunities to food retailers, though they will be hard pressed to gain substantial market shares. The strategy rests on the dubious assumption that the lure of one-stop shopping will revolutionise consumer shopping behaviour, whereas the evidence suggests that shoppers actively seek to separate grocery from other shopping. Both Tesco and Argyll acknowledge that shopping trips for food and clothing are separate occasions, while Marks & Spencer go further, admitting to different types of customer for food and for clothes (Salomon Bros 1991). Meanwhile, Asda's struggle to keep up with the other three major food retailers is attributed in part by city analysts to the firm's exposure to non-food markets (*The Times* 1991).

Some supermarkets are engaged in geographically based market development strategies within the UK with, for instance, Asda moving into the south, while Sainsbury moves into the north. A sign, perhaps, that the majors' continued quest for expansion in a market showing signs of saturation is obliging them to confront one another. Certainly many commentators, both academic and commercial, consider that the rate of superstore opening programmes and static food expenditure make saturation in grocery retailing inevitable (Killen and Lees 1988; Verdict Research 1990; Ogbanna 1989; Randall 1990; Treadgold 1990). In response to this, Duke (1991) uses market leakage analysis to identify a number of differentiation strategies by which he suggests that UK grocery retailers can compete in a post-saturation market. Duke makes some timely and interesting observations to help individual firms maintain a competitive edge in an overcrowded market. However, the inter-nationalisation of food retailing during the 1990s will require an added, more proactive dimension.

Doubts about the exportability of food retailing

For service companies, out-of-country expansion is never simply a case of exporting marginal product. They must actually go to the country, face the customer and produce the service. The commitment needed to undertake this, combined with the problems of sourcing, training and quality control mean that cross-border expansion involves greater risk for service than it does for manufacturing companies (Carman and Langeard 1980). Furthermore, van der Ster (1989) claims that food choice is simply too nationalistic for the export of store concepts to be successful in the short term. However, Segal-Horn and Davison (1990) dispute this, and Dawson et al (1988) have identified broad trends in shopping behaviour common to all European countries. Even van der Ster expects to see the eventual emergence of a 'Euro-lifestyle', leading to the development of pan-European store concepts.

Ultimately, the success of cross-border operations already undertaken by many European supermarkets must dispel the contention that food retailing does not export (see Figure 10.1).

Lack of European market opportunities

Many mainland European countries (notably the biggest markets of France, Italy and Germany but also Belgium) have restrictive land use laws, which serve to protect small shopkeepers (Dawson and Burt 1988). Therefore, supermarkets in those countries have been less successful than their British counterparts in increasing their market share at the expense of small shops and have instead been obliged to compete directly with their peers. For this and other reasons these markets have experienced fierce competition and a lack of development opportunities. As a result many major grocers in northern Europe have chosen to look outside their national borders for expansion.

British supermarket operators may well view mainland European markets with suspicion, especially when compared with the relatively favoured status they enjoy in their home market. Nevertheless, opportunities in Europe do exist. Treadgold (1989) observes, with particular reference to French domination of Spanish food retailing, that for an increasing number of retailers international development has become the favoured growth strategy. Consequently, a number of leading retailers from northern Europe are seeking to establish a presence in the relatively undeveloped retail markets of the south.

The Single European Market will become the 'home' market for all British businesses, and food retailers are no exception. By delaying their entry into mainland markets British supermarkets risk missing the windows of opportunity already being exploited by their competitors, and are in danger of being marginalised in the 10 per cent of the community's food market represented by the United Kingdom.

Better opportunities in the US market

Sainsbury does at least have an international presence, having acquired Shaws Supermarkets in the USA in the late 1980s. However, even in the USA, Sainsbury is dwarfed by European competitors (Table 10.3). For many British firms the choice of the US market for international expansion is frequently the result of a common (but misplaced) faith in export market selection based upon psychological proximity (Dichtl et al 1983). Misconceptions about cultural similarity have caused severe problems for British retailers in the difficult North American market, including such retailing stars as W H Smith, Sock Shop and Marks & Spencer. Hamill and Crosbie (1990) take the view that, although the US market may be attractive, British retailers should reduce their US orientation and concentrate on Europe in order to reap the benefits of the Single European Market.

Table 10.3   Turnover of some US food retailers in foreign ownership

Company	Country of origin	US turnover ($bn)
Tengelmann	Germany	10.0
Ahold	The Netherlands	6.0
Delhaize 'le Lion'	Belgium	3.8
Sainbury	UK	1.4

Source: Adapted from Treadgold (1990)

The profit gap between British and other EC retail food markets

The major attraction of the UK market is the very high margins achieved by the big food retailers. It follows that the much lower margins earned in the rest of the EC are a major short-term deterrent for the managers of any British supermarket which might consider emulating the export successes of supermarket operators from mainland Europe (see Table 10.1). However, it is argued that high margins are only achieved in Britain because the market is uncritical and consumers do not realise that they are paying high prices (*The Sunday Times* 1991). Consequently, a number of market analysts question whether the margins currently being achieved by British supermarkets are sustainable; recent reports suggest that the profitability bubble may already have burst and that the market share gains implicit in the big fours' current investment plans will have to be bought by price promotions, leading to lower returns. Furthermore, it is thought that that the Single European Market will result in an averaging of returns throughout the Community (Mintel 1991; Salomon Bros 1991; Corporate Intelligence Group 1990). Clearly, if margins in Britain are expected to drop to near the same level as those in the rest of the Community then, in the long term, lower returns are not a deterrent to European expansion by British grocers.

BALANCING THE RISKS AND OPPORTUNITIES

The major supermarkets are faced with radical changes in their operating environment which will result in a completely different set of opportunities and threats; and they do not appear to be adapting well. The primary long-term need of food retailers to establish themselves in the European Community market is being sacrificed to their short-term need to continue to earn the exceptionally high margins which are only available in Britain. However, attempts to continue in the same old way to gain margin and market share seem certain to accelerate the deterioration of the home market, if not into price war then into more price-based competition – the successful avoidance of which has done so much for supermarket margins. Furthermore, the opportunities identified by some British retailers in North America are illusory, being based upon an impression of psychological proximity which has caused even the best of them to make profound and damaging errors of judgement. Whether they choose to or not, British supermarkets will be operating in a Europe-wide market, within an increasingly internationalised industry. Consequently, none of the reservations which they have about competing in Europe is, in the long term, as dangerous as the risk which they run of missing out on the opportunities available in mainland European markets, and of becoming marginalised in one small corner of the Single European Market.

SUMMARY

The governor of the Bank of England has expressed the view that the successful British industries are those which have always operated in an international environment, and that those which failed in the past operated on the basis of a guaranteed and uncritical home market (*The Sunday Times* 1990). Unfortunately, supermarkets seem to fit the latter profile, having achieved years of profitable growth by taking market share from small shops in an economic, social and legal environment which heavily favoured the major chains, and which enabled them to avoid competing directly with each other. This situation has been exploited with considerable skill by the management of the big four supermarkets. But, as the internationalisation of food retailing gathers pace, the question which remains is whether such 'hothouse' conditions have resulted in soft growth, producing firms which are international in stature, but which have not been forged in the heat of international competition.

An uncritical home market has allowed British supermarkets to avoid price competition and persuade consumers to finance margins three or four times higher than international norms. The methods chosen to exploit this: increased services, improved store interiors, better locations and higher prices, are classic wheel of retailing 'trading up' strategies which have resulted in the opening up of a competitive flank to European competitors (Brown 1991). Significantly, both the EC food retailers currently entering the UK market are price-based, low-status, minimal-service, limited-product-offering competitors, who must be eagerly anticipating the possibilty of a price war triggered by overambitious expansion plans (Figure 10.3).

In a tougher, international environment the lucrative home market has become the Achilles heel for which the supermarkets must now pay. Accustomed to high, and increasing, profitability from the food retail sector the City will swiftly punish any company whose profits falter. Any supermarket which dared to accept the international norm for food retail margins, so as to strengthen its position in the EC while market opportunities still exist, would face the certainty of a depressed share price. In consequence the assets of the company would become available cheaply, and the likely result of such a far-sighted, proactive policy would be a predatory takeover (Eccles 1989). The supermarkets have therefore evolved a stay-at-home strategy which makes a virtue out of necessity. It is based upon the assumption that the favourable trading conditions of the last decade will carry on throughout the 1990s, enabling them to continue to simultaneously gain market share and improve profitability.

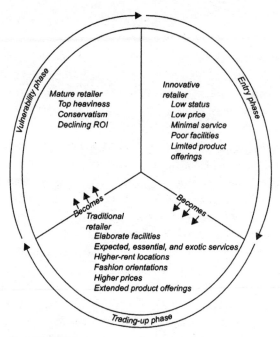

Source: Brown (1991)

Figure 10.3   The wheel of retailing

That scenario is extremely unlikely: the over-optimistic expansion plans of the big supermarkets are more likely to hasten market saturation, and lead to price-based competition and declining margins. The unfolding scenario resembles the space race in the stores sector during the 1980s. On that occasion also retailers added space to feed ambitious, and jointly incompatible, expansion plans, and were then surprised by the inevitable crash. Perhaps lulled by the inherent stability of the food sector, supermarkets do not appear to have heeded the warning.

The relatively favoured market situation enjoyed by British food retailers has spared them from the pressures which have driven many European competitors to seek markets abroad. However, this is a far from unmixed blessing, as failure to participate in European markets will eventually leave British food retailers in an untenable competitive position. Defence of the home market is simply not a winning strategy for British supermarkets because the UK retail food market is much smaller than those of Germany, Italy or France, and similar in value to that of Spain. Even a successful defence of the home market by supermarket operators would leave them isolated, niche operations confined to 10 per cent of the European market. Ultimately, they would be confronted by

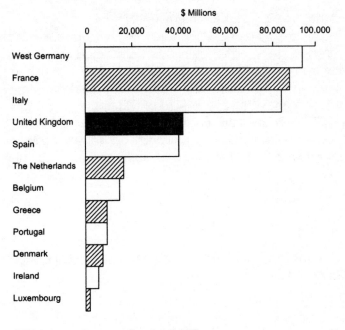

(1986 exchange rates – some figres include VAT)

Source: Euromonitor (1987).

Figure 10.4 Value of food markets – EC members

competitors which have grown and matured in a Europe-wide market ten times the size of their home market (Figure 10.4).

CONCLUSIONS

British business has had a difficult time in world markets over several decades, as is verified by the loss of world markets and a chronic balance of trade deficit. Successful industries have wilted under international competition. The current state of food retailing presents an example of a British industry which has been highly successful in the home market, and which is about to be tested in the international marketplace as the internationalisation of retailing gathers pace. In this chapter the opportunity has been taken to explore the response of food retailers to the imminent internationalisation of their industry, and finds them wanting. The findings are instructive, indicating that even such successful and well-managed British firms are faced with major in-built obstacles in the international arena. The uncritical nature of the UK market has not prepared the supermarkets for international markets any more than it did (say) the car manufacturers. Exceptionally high margins, available only in the UK, and the short-term requirements of institutional fund managers, effectively trap food retailers in the home market. The demands of the capital market lead the directors of British supermarkets to pretend that, if ignored, the Single European Market will go away. All this supports Doyle's (1988) argument that enforced financial orientation is a key factor in the continued difficulties experienced by British exporters, leading British managers to '...too often oversimplify the task and fail to sustain the long-term commitment required to sustain long-term competitive marketing performance'.

REFERENCES

Alexander N (1989), 'The Internal Market of 1992 – Attitudes of Leading Retailers', *Retail and Distribution Management*, Vol 16, 5, Jan/Feb.

Ansoff I (1957), 'Strategies for Diversification', *Harvard Business Review*, Sep/Oct.

Banque Paribas (1989), *The Outlook for UK and Continental Food Retailers*, Paribas Capital Markets Group, London.

Brown S (1991), 'Variations on a Marketing Enigma: The Wheel of Retailing Theory', *Journal of Marketing Management* Vol 7.

Carman J M and Langeard E (1980), 'Growth Strategies for Service Firms', *Strategic Management Journal*, Vol 1. pp 7–22.

Corporate Intelligence Group (1990), *Retail Research Report*, Dec, Corporate Intelligence Research Publications, London.

Dawson J A and Burt S (1988), *The Evolution of European Retailing*, The University of Stirling Institute for Retail Studies.

Dawson J A, Shaw S A and Rana J (1988), 'Future Trends in Food Retailing: Results of a Survey of Retailers', *British Food Journal* Vol 90, No 2, pp 51–7.

Debenham, Tewson and Chinnocks (1989), *1992 – The Retail Dimension*, London.

Delort J-J (1990), 'French Retailing and its Prospects Within 1993 Europe', *Marketing and Research Today*, Nov.

Dichtl E, Leibold M, Koglmayr H and Mueller S (1983) 'The Foreign Orientation of Management as a Central Construct in Export-Centred Decision Making Process', *Research for Marketing*, Vol 10, No 1.

Doyle P (1988), 'What Happened to Britain's Economic Miracle?', *The Director*, Apr.

Duke R (1991), 'Post Saturation Retailing in UK Grocery Retailing', *Journal of Marketing Management*, Vol 7.

Eccles T (1989), 'If We're so Smart, Why Are They Winning?' *Long Range Planning*, Vol 22, No 5.

Euromonitor (1987), 'Grocery Distribution in Western Europe', pp 24–5 and pp 31, Euromonitor Publications Ltd, London.

Grocer, The 1990, 21 Apr, p9.

Hamill J and Crosbie J (1990), 'British Retail Acquisitions in the US', *International Journal of Retail and Distribution Mangement*, Vol 18, No 5.

Killen V and Lees R (1988), 'The Future of Grocery Retailing in the UK part I', *Retail and Distribution Management* July/Aug.

— (1988), 'The Future of Grocery Retailing in the UK part II', *Retail and Distribution Management*, Nov/Dec.

Mintel (1991), *Retail Intelligence*, Vol 1, pp 10 and 13, Economist Intelligence Unit, London.

Nielsen A C (1990), *European Passport, a Strategic Assessment of the New Grocery Marketplace*, Oxford.

Ogbanna E (1989), 'Strategic Changes in UK Grocery Retailing', *Management Decision*, Vol 27, No 6.

Randall G (1990), *Marketing to the Retail Trade*, Heinemann, Oxford, pp 136–49.

Randlesome C , Brierly W, Bruton K, Gordon C and King P (1990), *Business Cultures in Europe*, Heinemann, Oxford, p 209.

Retail Week (1991), 19 Feb.

Salomon Bros (1991), 'UK Food Retailing', *UK Equity Research*, 26 April, London.

Segal-Horn S and Davison H (1990), 'Global Markets, the Global Consumer and International Retailing', working paper SWP41/90, Cranfield School of Management, Cranfield.

Sunday Times, The (1990), 22 April.

Sunday Times, The (1991), 11 Aug.

Super Marketing, 17 Aug, p3.

Super Marketing (1991), 29 Mar.

Thompson K E and Knox S (1991), 'The Single European Grocery Market: Prospects for a Channel Crossing', *European Management Journal*, Vol 9, No 1.

Times, The (1991), 1 Oct.

Treadgold A (1989), 'Pan-European Retail Business: Emerging Structure', *European Business Review*, Vol '89, No 4.

— (1990), 'The Developing Internationalisation of Retailing', *International Journal of Retailing and Distribution Management*, Vol 18, No 2.

van der Ster W (1989), 'Food Retailing in the 1990's: a Dutch View', *Proceedings of the Albert Heijn Conference*, Noordwijk, Koninlijke Ahold nv, Zaandam, Netherlands.

Verdict Research (1990), *The Space Report*, London.

Williams D E (1991) 'Retailer Internationalisation: Strategic Implications', *Proceedings of MEG Conference*, Cardiff.

11

HOW MANAGERS DEFINE CONSUMER MARKETS*

Mark Jenkins, Eric le Cerf and Thomas Cole

OUTLINE

This chapter explores the problem of defining markets in practice. The majority of current marketing literature places the customer as the sole element within a market; the purpose of the research outlined in this chapter is to explore how the marketing managers of major fast moving consumer goods organisations see their markets. The research categorises how a group of eighteen managers define their markets. The findings expose a heavy reliance on the market as a collection of products rather than customers: all the respondents included a product-based concept in their definition of market. A number of differing market maps were elicited which indicated that the majority of marketing managers (55 per cent) held broad market maps which integrated products, consumers and the marketing channel in an overall picture of the market. However, the remaining 45 per cent had relatively narrow market maps, with 11 per cent seeing the market and its segments only in terms of product concepts. The implications of this research are that managers need to be more explicit in how they define markets, as too narrow a definition may limit their perspectives at both the tactical and strategic levels. In addition, there is a need for further academic research to explore the subjectivity of market definitions within organisations.

The activity of marketing and the concept of the market are inextricably linked. In an organisational sense, the role of the marketing function is to understand and interpret the market to enable the organisation to achieve its corporate objectives. As the market is central to the activity of marketing, its definition and scope will determine the focus of the marketing activity. Levitt's seminal paper, 'Marketing Myopia' (1960),

---

* An earlier version of this chapter was presented at the Marketing Education Group 1993 conference, 'Emerging Issues in Marketing', Loughborough University Business School.

emphasises the importance of how organisations frame or define their markets. In discussing the demise of a US railroad company, Levitt considers that because they defined their market as railroads, rather than transportation, they lost customers by failing to appreciate the nature of the needs which they were satisfying. At an operational level, the importance of market definition is implicit in the array of marketing tools which are available to enhance the process of marketing management. Tools such as the Product Life Cycle (Cox 1967) and the Boston Matrix (Heldey 1977) all require input based on an objective and quantifiable market definition.

THE NATURE OF MARKET DEFINITIONS

A rudimentary scan through established marketing texts indicates that market definition is generally dealt with as a brief precursor to the intricacies of the marketing mix, marketing analysis and marketing strategy. Marketing theorists are relatively consistent in their position that the market is defined in terms of potential consumers, who are able to acquire products to satisfy particular needs or wants. Kotler (1991, p 8) provides an exemplary definition from the marketing literature:

> A market consists of all the potential customers sharing a particular
> need or want who might be willing and able to engage in exchange
> to satisfy that need or want.

Similar definitions to the above can be found in the majority of mainstream marketing texts. This view is further endorsed by the literature on market segmentation, the overall market definition being subdivided into identifiable sets of buyers, which are often given descriptors based on demographic or psychographic profiles (Tynan and Drayton 1987).

At the functional level, therefore, marketing theory defines markets as groups of customers. At a strategic level, market definition is used in a wider context and is central to the positioning of an organisation within the business environment. The concept of product/market linkages which connects the customer to the organisation's capabilities pervades the strategic management literature, for example Ansoff's product/market growth matrix (1965). In this concept of market definition, the customer is linked to the product and the technology used to create it. Abell (1980) uses three dimensions for defining the business in which an organisation operates: customer group; customer function; and the technological dimension, which defines how the customer's needs are being met.

Day (1981) identifies these differing perspectives for defining markets as top-down (strategic) and bottom-up (operational). The top-down perspective is concerned with competitive capability and resource transferability, the bottom-up with customer requirements and usage patterns. The implication of Day's framework is that market definition, rather than being a static concept, is likely to vary within the organisation at differing decision levels.

Market definition is a central concept in defining the organisation's domain, at both the operational and strategic levels. If market definition is such a central element in the way an organisation operates, what is known about how organisations define their markets? Curran and Goodfellow (1990) note the paucity of research in this area and, whilst economists have focused on this subject, there is still a lack of consensus as to how markets can or should be defined. If the theorists are unable to agree, what about the practitioners? It appears that in this regard, defining markets remains a highly problematic activity. Knight (1991) expresses the view that, in practice, the market definition used by organisations is a function of internal factors, such as the production process and organisational structure:

> The idea of markets should be a construct which enables us to simplify and therefore observe and predict consumer behaviour. The practice, however, too often reflects the companies' internal issues and history.

This is in contrast to the marketing literature, which focuses on external factors such as customer groupings and usage patterns. Evidently, there is a gap between this view of marketing practice and marketing theory. McDonald (1992) estimates that less than a quarter of UK companies utilise formal analysis techniques in the marketing planning process; one reason attributed to such a low rate of adoption being the problematic issue of defining the market in which they operate.

Market definition is, therefore, a paradoxical issue, at one level simplistic and at another apparently complex. It is frequently an issue which is taken for granted. Organisations believe it to be commonly understood and clearly defined, yet the evidence indicates that it is often misunderstood and likely to vary at differing organisational levels and contexts. Research in this area has tended to be normative or prescriptive and there is little evidence as to how organisations actually define their markets at different levels of decision making, and whether such definitions are reflected in the marketing theory.

INTERPRETIVE RESEARCH APPROACHES

Within the broader area of managerial research, there is a body of literature which appraises the impact of the perceptual process on managerial behaviour. Such research is broadly described as interpretive. It seeks to elicit how individuals interpret their environments. Interpretive management research has indicated that managers respond to increasing complexity with increased simplification (Duhaime and Schwenk 1985; Schwenk 1984), and that they may also bias, distort or filter stimuli to support their existing belief structures (Barnes 1984; Walsh 1988). If such interpretations affect the nature of marketing decision making, it is important that we understand how such managers interpret or define their markets.

Research has been undertaken in the strategic management area, to determine how managers interpret their competitive environments. Porac, Thomas and Baden-Fuller (1989) elicited the mental maps which managers hold of their competitors. This research revealed that managers tended to select only a limited number of firms against which they believed they were competing. Porac and Thomas (1990) describe such phenomena as, 'cognitive oligopolies'. Reger (1988) elicited the dimensions which managers were using to assess their competitors. This revealed a number of dimensions which were not evident in the literature, thus providing an indication that interpretive approaches to research may bring new understanding to managerial processes and behaviour.

With the exception of the work on competitors, there appears to have been little application of interpretive research approaches to determine how managers define their markets. Stubbart and Ramaprasad (1988) used cognitive mapping to explore the views of two industry leaders and identified differences in their maps in terms of reference to customers and international orientation. Dichtl et al (1983) use the concept of psychological distance to explain managers' orientation toward foreign investment, a concept which has been supported by more recent studies (Williams 1991). None of these studies, however, has attempted to assess the wider market definition within which organisations, or managers, define their area of operation.

INTERPRETIVE RESEARCH FOR DEFINING MARKETS

In order to investigate the issue of interpretive market definitions, the study in this chapter is guided by two research questions emanating from the current literature.

1. What type of market definition would we expect marketing managers to hold?

As managers working at an operational level, it would be reasonable to expect that marketing managers would see their markets as groups of potential customers. They are also likely to segment markets, on the basis of the characteristics of customers and their usage of the product. At strategic decision-making levels, it may be expected that technology and product issues would become further integrated into the market definition, as suggested by Abell (1980) and Day (1981).

2. Would we expect the nature of market definition to vary across industries?

The second question deals with the effects of different industries. It is an accepted view that industries tend to hold common sets of assumptions and beliefs. These have been termed industry recipes (Spender 1989). It can, therefore, be expected that organisations within an industry are likely to have common frameworks for defining their markets, ie there is an industry norm as to how the market is defined.

METHODOLOGY

A body of literature exists within the strategic management perspective, which attempts to construct interpretive frameworks of how managers make sense of their world. This methodology has been broadly termed 'cognitive mapping' (see Huff 1990 for an overview). The approach taken in this chapter is to attempt to map the cognitive frameworks which marketing managers hold for defining their markets. This will be undertaken by eliciting the categories of concepts which managers use to describe their markets. In order to do this, a conceptual framework is adopted to provide a protocol for the interviewing methodology. This is, firstly, to define the broad market in which they operate, ie the working parameters of the marketplace, and secondly to define the partitions within the market, ie the key segmentation variables which are being used.

As this study is essentially exploratory, an idiographic approach is used (Eden et al 1979). In this context, concepts are developed from the respondents and categorised following their elicitation. This is in contrast to using a structured approach, such as a questionnaire, which would involve presenting the respondent with a priori assumptions about the nature of market definition. Whilst this introduces a greater level of face validity to the data, as the respondent is using concepts and phrases with which he or she is comfortable, it increases the complexity and judgemental nature of the analysis.

The interviews were carried out by two of the authors. They followed a semi-structured interview format involving open-ended questions, followed by a prompting structure to move from the abstract (How would you define the term market?) to the more concrete (What are the important elements in your market?). The purpose of this format was to allow the respondents to use their own language and concepts, placing emphasis on reducing the input of the interviewer and maximising the output from the interviewee. The interviews lasted between 30 minutes and one hour and were recorded and transcribed for the purpose of analysis.

Sample

The largest 55 major companies from within both the food and brewing sectors were identified, using the *Kompass Directory*. Telephone calls were made to ascertain the identity of the marketing manager, or equivalent, and these were then sent a letter of introduction, explaining the nature of the research and requesting an interview. Following a series of follow-up phone calls, a total of eighteen interviews were completed with the marketing managers of nine organisations in the food sector and nine within the brewing sector.

Analysis

The analysis stage involved post hoc categorisation of the transcripts. All three researchers independently analysed the transcripts, using the framework outlined earlier, to categorise the concepts provided by the respondent. Further categories were developed based on the content of the transcript, ie free form categorisation (eg Reger 1988). Following independent coding, the transcripts were discussed across the three researchers, the purpose being to remove anomalies and provide an agreed framework for each respondent (Brown 1992).

RESULTS

1. What type of market definition would we expect market managers to hold?

As all the respondents had operational responsibility for the marketing decisions related to their company's or business unit's products, it was anticipated that the operational and functional nature of their position would mirror the view of the marketing literature, that markets were essentially groups of customers. In the discussion revolving around the respondent's broad understanding of the market, eight concept categories were identified. These are listed in Table 11.1.

Table 11.1 Concept categories for broad market definition

Market Concept	Frequency	% Respondents
Product	16	89
Channel	5	28
Consumer	3	17
Brands	2	11
Geography	2	11
Consumer function	2	11
Product volume	1	6
Packaging	1	6

The output of the analysis at the broad market definition level appears contrary to the view which dominates the marketing literature. The consumer, or the final customer, was only mentioned by three respondents, and consumer function mentioned by two. The dominant concept is product, which was identified in sixteen of the eighteen transcripts. In six transcripts, product was the only concept identified in the discussion on market definition, examples being the beer market and the wrapped sliced loaf market. This analysis provides an indication that the current theoretical descriptors of market definition are not being applied in practice. It also surfaces the concept of channel, or intermediary, as an important element in the way that these particular managers define their markets. In line with Abell's (1980) multi-dimensional approach to market definition, the majority of cases combined these concepts in some way: for example 'the food retail market' encompasses both product-based concepts and channel-based concepts; the leisure market for beer incorporates customer-function and product-based concepts. The only unitary grouping to occur was the product concept in isolation (six respondents).

Perhaps surprisingly, fewer concepts were identified at the segmentation level than at the broad market definition level. These are outlined in Table 11.2.

Table 11.2   Concept categories for defining market segments

Segment concept	Frequency	% Respondents
Channel (customer type)	13	72
Product characteristics	11	61
Consumer type	11	61
Consumer function	4	22
Geography	2	11
Level of branding	1	6

As can be seen from Table 11.2, there were three dominant concepts for segmenting the market: channel (eg on trade/off trade for the brewery sector, multiple or wholesale channels for the food sector); product characteristics (eg lagers/ales for the brewers, ambient/frozen for the food manufacturers); and consumer type (eg teenage/adult). Some of these were used in combination to produce segments defined by a number of these concepts. However, many respondents (seven) only used one of these concepts to define their market segments.

A further analysis was undertaken to combine the broad market and segmentation concepts into an integrated market map. These maps represent the overall categoric structure of their market definition. All the elements within the market maps generated can be categorised into product, channel or consumer concepts. The distribution of these concepts is outlined in Table 11.3. In overall terms, the market maps were dominated by product concepts, every respondent incorporating a product-based concept in their maps, whereas 28 per cent of these maps did not include a consumer-based concept.

Table 11.3   Overall concept categories within market map

Concept categories	Frequency	% Respondents
Product/channel/consumer	10	55
Product/channel	3	17
Product/consumer	3	17
Product	2	11

Two exemplars of such maps are shown in Figures 11.1 and 11.2. Figure 11.1 shows a three concept map, where the manager has integrated three concept groups: product, channel and consumer. In contrast, Figure 11.2

Market

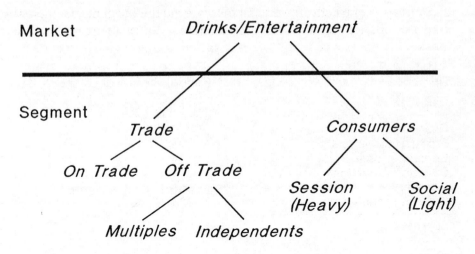

Figure 11.1 Example of tri-concept map (product, channel & consumer)

Market

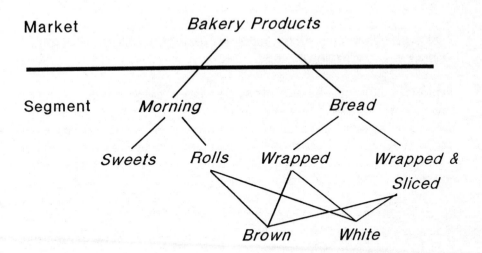

Figure 11.2 Example of uni-concept map (product)

illustrates a single concept map. In this case, all the concepts within the map are product-based descriptors. Analysis across all the market maps indicated a high level of idiosyncrasy at both the structural and content levels. Of the eighteen respondents, only three shared identical maps. This modal map is shown in Figure 11.3. It should be noted that the modal map does not contain any consumer concepts.

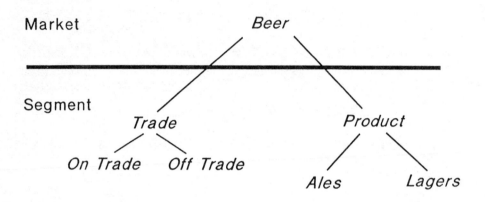

Figure 11.3 Modal scoring map (three respondents)

2 What differences exist between industry interpretations of market definition?

Table 11.4 illustrates the distribution of concept categories between the two industry sectors. Due to the small sample size, it is not possible to determine significant differences between these two sectors. At a descriptive level, they are broadly similar, with a noticeable difference in scores for the channel category, the brewing sector incorporating this concept into more of their individual maps. It is also of note that the modal map, illustrated in Figure 11.3, is provided by three marketing managers, all of whom work within the brewing sector. This tentative analysis indicates that product/channel concepts may be dominant in the market definitions of the brewing sector, and this is perhaps due to the level of vertical integration within this particular industry. The general implication is that there may be industry norms for the market maps, which are explained by the structure and nature of particular industries.

Table 11.4 Concept categories by industry sector

Concept	Brewing	Food
Product	9 (100%)	9 (100%)
Channel	8 (89%)	5 (56%)
consumer	7 (78%)	6 (67%)

CONCLUSIONS

The output of this research supports the view that there is a disparity between the way in which markets are defined in the marketing literature, and the way in which they are defined in practice. The product concept dominated the market definitions elicited from this group of marketing managers. Every respondent included a product-based concept at the broad or segment level of their market definition. In contrast, 28 per cent of the respondents had no consumer-, or final customer-, based concepts within their view of the market.

The question which this finding raises is whether the product concept is dominant, because these managers define their market at a strategic level, and therefore include the resource-based concepts outlined by Abell (1980) and Day (1981), or whether they are displaying a product orientation, and suffering from the myopia which Levitt (1960) observed. The research also indicates that further concepts for defining markets, which are not emphasised in the literature, may be obtained through interpretive studies of this type. The importance of the channel concept in the context of the brewing industry was identified through the elicitation of the market maps.

The implications for managers are that they need to develop a clearer appreciation of their own, individual market definitions. What definitions do they implicitly utilise in their decision making? Is such a definition appropriate for the range of decisions which they need to make? Is market definition taken for granted in their organisation? Do marketing teams, or sales teams share similar market definitions or are they, as was the case in this study, highly variable across individuals?

For researchers, further work is required to determine the relationship between market definitions and types of decisions, in order to understand the possible dynamics and variability of market definition. A further dimension is to understand the organisational or social aspects of market definition. Is there an organisational definition which determines the way the organisation sees the marketing environment, or are they idiosyncratic frameworks which will vary greatly within organisations?

This research is exploratory and has therefore tended to raise questions rather than answer them. These questions, however, are fundamental to our understanding of the evident gap between marketing theory and marketing practice.

Acknowledgement

The authors would like to thank Professor Malcolm H B McDonald for his invaluable comments on an earlier draft of this chapter. Opinions expressed and conclusions drawn are, however, the sole responsibility of the authors.

REFERENCES

Abell D F (1980), *Defining the Business: The Starting Point of Strategic Planning*, Prentice-Hall, Engelwood Cliffs, NJ.

Ansoff H I (1965), *Corporate Strategy*, McGraw-Hill, New York.

Barnes J H Jr (1984), 'Cognitive Biases and Their Impact on Strategic Planning', *Strategic Management Journal*, 5, pp 129–37.

Brown S M (1992), 'Cognitive Mapping and Repertory Grids for Qualitative Survey Research: Some Comparative Observations', *Journal of Management Studies*, 29, 3, pp 287–308.

Cox W E Jr (1967), 'Product Life Cycles as Marketing Models', *Journal of Business*, Oct, pp 375–85.

Curran J G M and Goodfellow J H (1990), 'Theoretical and Practical Issues in the Determination of Market Boundaries', *European Journal of Marketing*, 24, 1, pp 16–28.

Day G S (1981), 'Strategic Market Analysis and Definition: An Integrated Approach', *Strategic Management Journal*, 2, pp 281–99.

Dichtl E, Leibold M, Koglmayr H G and Muller S (1983), 'The Foreign Orientation of Management as a Central Construct in Export-centred Decision-making Processes', *Research for Marketing*, 10, 1, pp 7–14.

Duhaime I M and Schwenk C R (1985), 'Conjectures on Cognitive Simplification in Acquisition and Divestment Decision Making', *Academy of Management Review*, 10, 2, pp 287–95.

Eden C, Jones S and Sims D (1979), *Thinking in Organizations*, Macmillan, London.

Heldey B (1977), 'Strategy and the Business Portfolio', *Long Range Planning*, Feb, p 12.

Huff A S (1990), *Mapping Strategic Thought*, Wiley, Chichester.

Knight D (1991), 'A Problem of Market Definition', *Marketing*, 25 July, p 17.

Kotler P (1991), *Marketing Management: Analysis Planning and Control*. 7th edition, Prentice-Hall, Engelwood Cliffs, NJ.

Levitt T (1960), 'Marketing Myopia', *Harvard Business Review*, July–Aug, pp 45–56.

McDonald M H B (1992), 'Strategic Marketing Planning: A State-of-the-art Review', *Marketing Intelligence and Planning*, 10, 4, pp 4–22.

Porac J F and Thomas H (1990), 'Taxonomic Mental Models in Competitor Definition', *Academy of Management Review*, 15, 2, pp 224–40.

Porac J F, Thomas H and Baden-Fuller C (1989), 'Competitive Groups as Cognitive Communities: The Case of the Scottish Knitwear Manufacturers', *Journal of Management Studies*, 26, 4, pp 397–416.

Reger R K (1988), 'Competitive Positioning in the Chicago Banking Market: Mapping the Mind of the Strategist', unpublished PhD thesis, University of Illinois at Urbana-Champaign.

Schwenk C R (1984), 'Cognitive Simplification Processes in Strategic Decision Making', *Strategic Management Journal*, 5, pp 111–28.

Spender J C (1989), *Industry Recipes: The Nature and Sources of Management Judgement*, Basil Blackwell, Oxford.

Stubbart C I and Ramaprasad A (1988), 'Probing Two Chief Executives' Schematic Knowledge of the US Steel Industry Using Cognitive Maps', *Advances in Strategic Management*, 5, pp 139–64.

Tynan A C and Drayton J (1987), 'Market Segmentation', *Journal of Marketing Management*, 2, 3, pp 301–35.

Walsh J P (1988), 'Selectivity and Selective Perception: An Investigation of Managers' Belief Structures and Information Processing', *Academy of Management Journal*, 31, 4, pp 873–96.

Williams D E (1991), 'Retailer Internationalisation: Strategic Implications', *Marketing Education Group Conference Proceedings*, Cardiff, pp 1339–60.

12

STRATEGY SEARCH AND CREATIVITY; THE KEY TO CORPORATE RENEWAL*

Simon Majaro

OUTLINE

In common with most functional disciplines in the managerial firmament, marketing has become a complex process. Have we allowed it to become too complex? I often feel that in the academic world we admire the complex and despise the simple. From across the Atlantic the very simplistic response is expressed in the primitive notion of KISS (Keep it Simple Stupid. . .). To serious people this expression verges on a caricature of a concept. Yet it encompasses a powerful indictment of the way academics and contemporary thinkers and researchers often lose sight of the importance of grappling with complex challenges in simple and easily decodable messages.

The aim of this chapter is to simplify important concepts and to make them practical and implementable.

The important point to bear in mind, at all times, is that marketing does not and cannot live alone. The organisation that allows the marketing function (or any other function) to drift apart from a holistic and well-integrated federation of activities will never attain excellence. Marketing may well be the locomotive that pulls the rest of the organisation towards corporate goals. Nevertheless it must be remembered that in a truly customer/consumer-orientated organisation all functions must think about the customers and their requirements in a steadfast way. It is a simple philosophy which, if implemented in a robust manner, can yield rich awards.

Thus, I start from the simple proposition that success depends on the total appreciation by everybody in the firm of the need to satisfy

---

* This chapter first appeared in *European Management Journal*, Vol 10, No 2, June 1992.

customers. All members of an organisation must talk, think and act with customers' needs and expectations in mind at all times. What is good for the customer is good for the business. This philosophy must pervade not only all functions but also all levels. The 'people at the top' must also remember that what they do in the search for strategies, and in the development of missions and their underlying philosophies, must adhere to the fundamental concept that customers must be satisfied by everything that emanates from the top.

It is within this context that I have been researching the role of creativity and innovation in organisations. Indisputably, creativity and innovation are the secret ingredients which can help to turn a suboptimal performance into an excellent one. When these two ingredients are directed towards satisfying consumers and their needs, the output is almost assured of success. This is a simple enough concept, yet many company strategists think that creativity is an activity that belongs to lower levels of management. It is quite common to observe top managers who cajole and exhort their subordinates to generate creative ideas but refuse to participate in the process themselves. The main aim of this chapter is to alert top management to the role they can play in the task of promulgating a more creative organisation.

The use of creativity in the search for strategy can provide a powerful stimulus to a more innovative company and that, in turn, can enhance the firm's ability to satisfy its consumers in a more consistent way. In other words, creativity and innovation are not an end in themselves. They represent the cutting edge that can help firms to renew themselves and manage change in a visionary fashion.

INTRODUCTION

Top management is often heard to invite people in the organisation to become more creative. Some enlightened companies go so far to invest in the process of educating and training members of the organisation in how to become more creative. Yet very few leaders of industry and commerce actually indulge themselves in creative activities. Creativity is regarded as a desirable pattern of behaviour for *others* to pursue. Those who have reached the top of the hierarchical ladder somehow believe that 'creativity' is something one can delegate to other members of the firm. A very illustrious captain of industry once told me, in unequivocal terms: 'I pay people high salaries to do their job and that includes being creative'.

There follows a little checklist for those belonging to the strategic level of the firm:

1. When did you last participate in a creative session designed to solve problems and/or explore new opportunities? Yes No

2. Have you taken part in a brainstorming session (or any other session utilising creative techniques) since you got to your top position? Yes No

3. Have you ever reflected upon the barriers that stand in the way of your firm's ability to improve its creativity and innovation? Yes No

4. When planning the future of your company, do you attempt to use creative methods in coalescing a vision of the future? Yes No

5. When developing the firm's mission, do you:
   (a) Use creative methods to identify the most relevant statement within the firm's circumstances? Yes No
   (b) Insert a statement about creativity being part of the firm's culture? Yes No

6. Do you go out of your way to ensure that ideas flow from:
   (a) Personnel inside the firm? Yes No
   (b) From the international environment? Yes No

7. Do you take steps to motivate people to be creative? Yes No

8. Do you monitor the firm's level of creativity and innovation in a systematic way? Yes No

If senior managers respond to any of these questions with a 'No', they ought to reflect very seriously about their contribution to the firm's creative processes and identify the role which they propose to play in enhancing creativity and innovation in the organisation. The one point that top management should always remember is that they are often a role model for managers at lower levels. The boss who stifles everybody's ideas cannot expect members of the organisation to behave differently. On the other hand, the chief operating officer who grasps every idea with open arms provides a powerful stimulant to the generation of ideas and their communication throughout the firm.

I have been involved in helping firms to become more creative and more innovative for many years, and in many parts of the world. During the last five years, I and a number of colleagues from one of the leading business schools started applying the principles of creative thinking towards the search for company strategy and the development of corporate plans. In other words, we have been seeking to inject creativity at the strategic level of the firm. In common with most consultants/academics, we have had our share of successes and failures. Nonetheless, valuable lessons were learnt from both and in this chapter I wish to summarise a few of these lessons.

BACKGROUND CONCEPTS

I always start my explorations in the field of creativity and innovation by defining my terms. Experience has taught me that although the two words 'creativity' and 'innovation' are being used in the business world with great frequency, communication is often hampered by the fact that different people ascribe different meanings to these two words. When I ask ten managers on a workshop to describe their understanding of these two terms, I usually receive ten different definitions.

I use the two terms in the following way:

- *Creativity* is the thinking process which helps us to generate ideas
- *Innovation* is the application of an idea towards doing things better, cheaper, more aesthetically and/or more effectively.

An idea can be bizarre, outlandish, wild or even useless. On the other hand, an innovation has to be useful, results orientated, profitable or effective. Why waste time on outlandish ideas? The reason is simple: without ideas one is unlikely to attain innovations. Moreover, history has shown that one needs many ideas to feed the innovation process. As many as 60 ideas are needed before a successful innovation is attained. In other words, a firm that deprives itself of the input generated by the creative process will find that it starves itself of the desirable task of innovating. Creativity per se does not amount to much. It is purely the 'input' which facilitates the attainment of innovation – the 'output'. We need people's creativity because without it we are not likely to achieve the level of innovation which makes our organisations more effective, more productive and more successful. Figure 12.1 illustrates the relationship between creativity and innovation.

On the whole, top management understands this simple truth. However, there is normally a gap between what management believes in and what actually happens at lower levels. Top management people, or as I prefer to call the people at the top, the 'strategic level', often prefer to exhort others to 'become more creative and more innovative', but do not want to become involved in the process of changing attitudes and leading

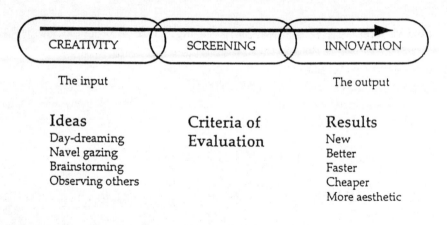

| CREATIVITY | SCREENING | INNOVATION |

The input   The output

Ideas   **Criteria of**   **Results**
Day-dreaming   **Evaluation**   New
Navel gazing   Better
Brainstorming   Faster
Observing others   Cheaper
                                                   More aesthetic

Source: Majaro, *Managing Ideas for profit*, McGraw Hill, 1992

Figure 12.1 The relationship between creativity and innovation

the task of developing the kind of shared values that enhance the firm's creativity and innovation demands. Bosses who abdicate from this vital task cannot expect the organisation to become truly creative and ultimately innovative.

For those who recognise the importance of developing a more creative organisation, the integrated approach to creativity and innovation described in Figure 12.2 is a useful starting point. A number of elements

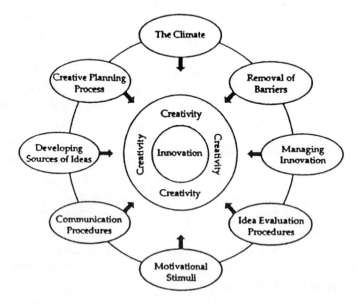

Source: Majaro (1991)

Figure 12.2 Creativity and innovation – an integrated approach

must by in place if the whole process of innovation can be managed in a cohesive and well-structured manner. Eight elements are shown and a brief description of each one of them will help to place this model in its proper context.

Climate

The climate for innovation is right when every person in the firm – senior or junior – 'thinks', 'talks', 'dreams' and 'acts' creatively. In other words, innovation becomes an integral part of the firm's culture and *shared values*: an easy concept to talk about; a daunting task to achieve. It calls for a persistent and imaginative programme of work, masterminded from the top but implemented at all levels.

Creative planning process

As emphasised earlier, innovation must start at the top; the bosses must demonstrate their ability to develop an innovative vision and plan the future direction of the firm in a creative way. This particular element will form the main thrust of this chapter.

Removal of barriers

Every firm suffers from a number of barriers that impede the flow of ideas. These barriers differ from company to company although obstacles such as bureaucracy, the 'not invented here' syndrome and 'bean-counting' exist in many organisations. Top management of every company should 'audit' the specific barriers that interfere with the creativity of their respective organisations and seek to remove them. (For further details, see Majaro 1992.)

Developing sources of ideas

Ideas can be tapped from inside the firm (eg through suggestion schemes or the use of idea-generation techniques) and from outside sources (eg customers, consultants, competitors, different industries). The options are multifarious, but active steps must be undertaken to develop a systematic approach to harnessing them. (See Von Hippel 1988.)

Communication procedures

People in any organisation have ideas or observe interesting innovations in the external environment. A system must be established to ensure that every member of the organisation knows how and to whom to convey such ideas. Communication procedures do not happen by themselves. This is particularly true in the context of multi-national organisations. Companies operating in a number of countries have an opportunity to benefit from the cross-fertilisation of ideas emanating from different environments and cultures. Failure to exploit such a rich seam of ideas almost negates the value of being multi-national. Figure 12.3 illustrates the two ways in which ideas can flow in a multi-national context. Clearly, the systematic way described in the second model is the one that a company should strive to develop. (See Majaro 1988.)

Motivational stimuli

Members of the organisation can easily become more creative when they know that their input is appreciated. Such stimuli need not be of a financial or material nature. A symbol of recognition can often have a more potent impact than a monetary reward.

Idea evaluation procedures

Let us assume that the firm has organised itself to tap people's ideas and/or generate a myriad of ideas through the many techniques that exist for that purpose. The ability to screen and evaluate such ideas promptly and efficiently is a most powerful tool in the whole process. One of the killers of creativity is the inability to convert ideas into reality in a systematic fashion.

Managing innovation

The innovative company must establish a system for monitoring and controlling the level of innovation that has been achieved during a given period. The best stimulus to creativity is the knowledge that ideas are being implemented from time to time. Moreover, the system should highlight the lessons learnt from recent successes and failures.

Figure 12.4 provides one example of the kind of controlling procedures which I have been inviting my clients to maintain in this regard. Many other monitoring procedures can be developed in response to the specific needs of each organisation.

In summary, there are eight highly interrelated elements which must be developed and put in place by top management if the firm is to become

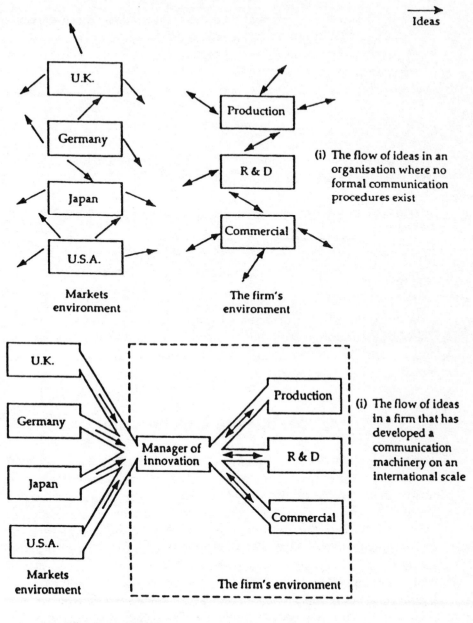

Ideas

(i) The flow of ideas in an organisation where no formal communication procedures exist

Markets environment

The firm's environment

(i) The flow of ideas in a firm that has developed a communication machinery on an international scale

Markets environment

The firm's environment

The flow of ideas
(i) in firms without formal idea communication procedures
(i) in firms that have developed a machinery for communicating ideas on a global scale

Source: Majaro (1988)

Figure 12.3 The systematic flow of ideas in a multi-national context

Innovation number	Description of Innovation	Date Implemented	Benefits attained (over period to be specified)	Further work needed	Lessons learned

Source: Majaro (1991)

Figure 12.4 Innovation analysis worksheet

more creative and, in turn, increase its ability to become more innovative. They are all important and they must all be pursued with steadfastness and imagination. Nevertheless, in this chapter I want to dwell on the 'creative planning process', as it was in this area we discovered rich pickings.

STRATEGY SEARCH AND CREATIVITY

Top management of most companies realise that their businesses operate in an environment which is more complex, more dynamic and more hostile than ever. Competitive pressures have increased, technology is shortening product lifecycles and customer requirements are becoming more sophisticated. The challenge is how to manage such an environment within the context of existing corporate resources in a more creative way. Moreover, how can we move towards a management style which anticipates these changes rather than reacts to them? To use the language of the modern planner – how can we become proactive rather than reactive in our corporate behaviour. Clearly, being proactive also calls for a measure of creative thinking.

Together with a number of colleagues at my business school, we developed a structured approach to the search for strategies. We call the process 'strategy search'. It is a systematic step-by-step process aimed at identifying the options available to the company in its search for the most appropriate future direction. It is an informal gathering of senior managers and decision makers (usually no more than a dozen) from one organisation, in a pleasant environment, in which major strategic issues can be ventilated. During a short period of two or three days, and away from the normal workplace, the group explores and evaluates, together with two independent and experienced strategic thinkers, the most viable and innovative route which the company could pursue.

Through the use of a number of specially devised techniques and aids to creative thinking, the participants are encouraged to appraise objectively the threats and opportunities that their organisation is facing and to recognise the company's most significant strengths and weaknesses. The outcome of this analysis provides the starting point for the development of successful product/market strategies.

Our facilitators who run the 'strategy search' meetings are all experienced in providing unobtrusive direction to the discussions. They are also well versed in the use of methods and techniques associated with the management of creativity. By bringing senior managers together in an informal environment, and by following a number of well-tried processes, our approach can yield good results in a short period of time.

The kind of topics that fall within the orbit of a 'strategy search' programme are as follows:

Developing a vision

The role of the strategic planning process is to lead the firm towards the future. This requires long-term perspectives. Short-term orientation does not lead to competitive advantage and continual self-renewal. The process of developing a vision helps management to gain a deeper awareness of its values, and that in turn helps to hone a set of values which are empathetic to the needs of the future. When vision and values are in harmony, a compelling desire to act is aroused. Thus, if the vision points at a 'greener' world, it forces us to reflect upon our role in such an environment and respond to the challenges prescribed by such a world.

The tool we use for this activity is a well-structured exercise in 'scenario daydreaming'. Unlike 'scenario writing', the visioning process takes place verbally. It is like a brainstorming session but relates to the group's imaging of the world at a given date in the future, say the year 2000. Each individual is allocated a factor for explanation such as economic trends, politics, ecology, cost of commodities. Topics for exploration are often allocated in accordance with people's specific knowledge and/or expertise. The important thing is that the discussions are centred around the concept that 'today is January 2000 and this is what is happening in the world around us . . .'. The use of the future tense must be avoided. A scribe records the main issues that emerge and through an iterative process the vision is refined and the implications for the company explored in some depth. Clearly, the collective knowledge of those present can enrich the value of the deliberations.

If one remembers that the most important point about planning is the process itself rather than the outcome, this vision development exercise can be a most potent generator of ideas for further reflection and analysis.

Developing a mission

'What is the purpose of our firm?' Defining the mission of the firm is a popular pastime. Many firms feel that without an elegant mission statement they have not earned their spurs. Once again, it is worth remembering that it is not the elegance of the mission statement which guarantees corporate excellence. It is the quality of knowledge and intellectual input which has gone into the process which provides the company with its cutting edge on the competitive scene. In this connection, we always emphasise the fact that a sound mission statement should avoid encompassing too many fancy and meaningless phrases. It should fulfil a number of basic and logical dimensions.

- Be specific enough to have an impact upon the behaviour of individuals throughout the business
- Be focused more on customer need/satisfaction
- Be based on an objective recognition of the company's strengths and weaknesses
- Recognise the opportunities and threats in the competitive environment
- Be realistic and attainable
- Be flexible.

(For more details see Christopher *et al* 1987.)

A good mission statement is the banner under which the firm will be operating. If carefully defined and refined, it inevitably projects the firm's set of shared values. These in turn reflect the firm's climate and culture.

During the search for a suitable mission we use techniques like brainstorming, trigger sessions, metaphorical analogy and brain patterns. More recently, we started using IdeaFisher, one of the computer software packages designed to augment one's idea-generation activities.

Identifying and developing 'shared values'

We have learnt during the last decade how important it is for a company to articulate a set of 'values' which are universally known among the company personnel and wholeheartedly shared. Once the vision and the mission have been coalesced, the key 'values' which may be instrumental for the attainment of excellence should be highlighted and built into the firm's ethos, code of behaviour and management development plans. These are the 'shared values' that distinguish an outstanding company from the rest.

Our favoured technique in this regard is metaphorical analogy or synectics. The ability to draw inspiration from analogous successes in other areas of human endeavour world wide and in history can be of great help.

Managing change

At this stage, top management often realises that managing change is becoming a major task. A vision leads to a mission and a mission helps to highlight the shared values that could be instrumental for future success. Clearly, this involves the firm in cultural changes which demand a creative input from both top management and those responsible for management development and training.

We find that the use of metaphorical analogy can be a powerful stimulant to the process of planning for and managing change. Through freewheeling sessions we seek to identify organisations, from any sphere of human activity, including religious creeds and political bodies, that have succeeded in indoctrinating a large number of people in the value of their beliefs. Changing an organisation from a production-orientated mode to a marketing-orientated creed bears some similarity with the way the early Christians have propagated their beliefs. Successes and failures of this nature can provide a powerful stimulus to the creative thinking of the participants.

Develop a 'sustainable competitive advantage'

Sooner or later, the board of directors must address itself to the task of attempting to develop a sustainable competitive advantage for the firm and its products and services. There is no need to stress here the importance of this activity. We all know that the winners of the 1990s will be those companies that manage to differentiate their offerings from their competitors. In marketing terms, innovation often entails differentiation and differentiation requires creative leaps. In this context, we use the 'strategic leap' method specifically devised for the purpose, and also such techniques as 'attribute listing' and brainstorming.

New product exploration and/or development

This is a logical culmination of the 'strategy search' cycle. Having started with vision development, one is bound to reach a point at which the participants want to consider practical ways to enrich the product portfolio for the future. A plethora of fun techniques exist to assist the group in exploring potential new products or product enhancements. Morphological analysis, attribute listing and brain patterns are useful methods in this connection. (For details of the techniques mentioned see Majaro 1991.)

These are some of the issues that are explored during 'strategy search' workshops. The important point to remember is that top management must tackle issues and problems relating to strategy, business direction and proactive anticipation of events. All these areas can benefit from creative thinking as much as any other operational problem can.

So far this does not represent a major breakthrough in the field of creativity and innovation. All that I have tried to highlight is the importance of applying well-tried techniques, and methods that we all associate with problem solving and exploratory creativity, towards assisting the company's top management in charting a course to the future.

MAJOR LESSONS LEARNED

'Strategy search' as a spur to creativity throughout the firm

The important revelation that we stumbled across almost 'by serendipity' is the fact that when a board of directors agrees to undertake a 'strategy search' session, they provide a most powerful spur to creativity throughout the firm. The news that the bosses are 'playing the creative game' in the pursuit of an innovative vision, mission and strategy is more potent than a massive programme of management development designed to enhance a climate in which creativity can spawn.

With this thought in mind, we have started to reverse the process: when top management ask us to help to stimulate creativity in the firm, we recommend that they, the people at the top, agree to participate in a well-publicised 'strategy search' creativity-orientated workshop. When I say 'well-publicised', I do not mean that the details of the deliberation should be communicated. It is the style of the programme, the method used and the aims sought which ought to be communicated. People lower down the organisation are bound to decode the message in an unequivocal way: 'If the bosses are playing the creative game we ought to do the same'. The impetus for learning about the creative processes which starts at the top becomes all pervasive and translates itself into a bottom-up pressure for a sustained effort at promulgating a more creative climate. We all tend to model ourselves on the way our leaders behave. A chairman of one of my client companies has recently started to arrive at work on a mountain bike. It is fascinating to watch the growth in number of such bikes in the firm's car park! Similarly, if the strategic level indulges in creative sessions, it does not take long for the rank and file to pursue similar activities. In other words, what has started as an exercise designed to help the firm to formulate strategies has proved to have much wider developmental spin-offs, albeit by association rather than by design.

The need for a holistic approach to strategy

The most significant lesson that we learnt from this experience is the importance for top management to look at 'creativity and innovation' as components in a complex framework of interrelated elements. Stimulating creativity out of context is unlikely to turn a poor enterprise into an excellent one. It may simply help the firm to 'do the wrong things better'. This is the subtle difference between efficiency and effectiveness. Creativity should be the tool that helps the firm to become more effective and not just more efficient. A *holistic* approach is required if the input of creative thinking is to play a contributing role in the pursuit of long-term success. This is a vital point which is often missed by top management. The myth still persists that all one needs to do is exhort people to be more creative or train them in idea-generation techniques and all will be well with the world.

Business gurus' books attempt to tell us about the panaceas for corporate excellence. Michael Porter (1985) has taught us about the value of 'competitive advantage'; Gifford Pinchot in *Intrapreneuring* has attempted to explain why big business, despite spending most of the world's R&D money, has a disproportionately small share of major innovations. In the highly fashionable field of quality, people like Demming, Crosby *et al* tell us all about the importance of getting the quality right, almost to the exclusion of everything else; Peters and Waterman, in the *In Search of Excellence*, have attempted to view excellence from a holistic vantage point, but unfortunately the book has too much pretence to balanced research. The one guru who always appears to view businesses in a holistic fashion is Peter Drucker. This is probably the main reason his books have survived the test of time.

In spite of all my research into the literature on the subject of creativity and innovation, I have not found any definitive paradigm that can guide us towards a better understanding of the exact role that top management can play in promulgating more innovative and more successful enterprises. My own proposition is based on empirical observation of company strategists during 'strategy search' workshops and an attempt at getting back to basics.

The proposition is based on a very simple axiom: *the success of any business depends on its ability to satisfy the customer.* Companies that fail to satisfy their customers are not likely to survive. The whole panoply of the marketing function is designed to assist us in fulfilling this fundamental task. 'Come close to the customer' is one of the prescriptions of Peters and Waterman in their book *In Search of Excellence*. So far so good, but the whole concept begs many questions:

1. *Who are the customers and what exactly are their needs?*
2. *Are we talking about today's customers or those of the future?* Clearly, looking at the firm from the vantage point of the strategic level, one has to accept that the future may be different from the present in many respects. To that extent, developing a vision, mission and strategy is an essential part of good top management.
3. *Who is responsible for satisfying the customer?* Is this purely the job of marketing personnel or should this be a company-wide process? The obvious answer is that it must be part of the total firm's ethos and shared values. Once again, top management must be a prime mover in inculcating such a creed.
4. *What 'knowledge' do we require to understand what would satisfy the customer now and in the future?* It is almost a cliché to say that we live in an era in which 'knowledge' is one of the prime assets of any organisation. According to a story, Einstein was once asked how he would spend his final hour in the face of mortal danger. His answer was: 90 per cent of that hour would be spent on collecting information; 5 per cent on weighing up alternative courses of action; the final 5 per taking a decision. The whole world of information technology is at

management's disposal. Is top management spending enough time exploring its value to the firm? One must remember that the essence of information is 'knowing what one needs to know'. Information per se is of limited value.

5. *Do the customers values our creativity?* The answer must be a loud 'yes' if our creativity leads to an innovation which provides the customers with a better and/or less costly and/or more aesthetic benefit or utility. Rare would be the customer who would not bless 3M for its development of 'Post-it' or Glaxo for its Zantac innovation. Both are successful and few would dispute the fact that creativity and innovation were major factors in the success.

Figure 12.5 summarises this holistic approach to an effective and creative top management philosophy. It aims to highlight the role that creativity and innovation can play in the whole process. The model described represents the main tasks of top management. They do not have to 'run' each of the activities encompassed in the satellites shown, but they certainly must reflect upon and initiate and mastermind the appropriate development programmes of work envisaged by each of them.

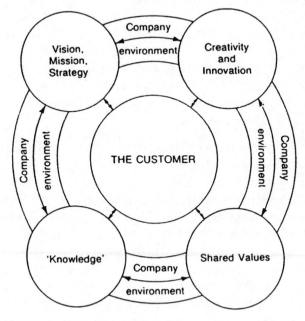

© Strategic Management Learning

Figure 12.5 Satisfying the customer – the company's 'input': a holistic approach

If 'the customer is king', the four satellites shown must work in total harmony within the company's environment, present and future, with the view of promulgating all the appropriate 'satisfiers' that would keep him or her happy, and such happiness should maintain the enterprise's overall success.

It is hoped that the model shown in Figure 12.5 is capable in itself of providing the reader with a framework for reflection and analysis pertaining to his or her business environment. It must be recalled that my aim is to highlight the strategic context within which 'creativity and innovation' can act as a powerful spur to a longer term excellence. Two important points must be emphasised.

1. The model described is only relevant in the context of firms that have accepted the validity of being marketing orientated. Obviously, companies that are still resisting the 'marketing concept' are fighting gravity and are not likely to achieve corporate renewal. All the evidence gleaned during our 'strategy search' workshops has reinforced our long-held conviction that companies that refuse to move towards a customer-led or marketing-led mode are gambling with their future. Market conditions are such that the punishment for those who refuse to grapple with change is likely to be severe.
2. The four elements shown in Figure 12.5 must be viewed as an integrated assemblage. They interact, enrich and fertilise each other. Creativity enhances visioning and visioning, in turn, stimulates creativity. A shared vision has the potential of being an integrating force in the organisation, culminating in a set of shared values to which people can feel fully committed.

Creativity and innovation must become part of the firm's shared values if they are to become part of the organisation's cutting edge. When 3M talk about the '25 per cent Rule' they invite all managers to analyse their product portfolio and ensure that, at all times, at least 25 per cent of the products under their control are less than five years old! The message is clear: 'you must invest time in creativity in order to innovate'. This in turn becomes an integral part of the firms' shared values. Members of the organisation 'talk', 'think' and 'act' innovation. It is part of the firm's creed.

'Knowledge' is another powerful catalyst that can enrich the company's efforts at satisfying the customer. (See Oliff and Marchand 1991.) It is outside the scope of this chapter to enumerate all the areas in which effective knowledge management or information management can provide the company with a powerful competitive advantage. Suffice it to emphasise with the paradigm described in Figure 12.5 that a company that acquires more accurate, more comprehensive and more anticipatory knowledge than its own customers possess is in a pretty strong position in the competitive world we live in. Customers will gravitate towards such a supplier!

'Knowledge' can enrich the vision, mission and strategy development processes. All can gain enormously from the support of a team that adheres to a cohesive and unified set of values. All three can be spurred by creativity. A firm that manages to slot creativity into such a holistic framework will be the winner of the 1990s. Obviously, this can only be achieved at the instigation of the firm's top leadership.

References

Adams J D (ed) (1986), *Transforming Leadership: From Vision to Results*, Miles River Press, Alexandria, VA.

Christopher M, Majaro S and McDonald M (1987), *Strategy Search*, Gower, Aldershot.

Lamb R B (1984), *Competitive Strategic Management*, Prentice-Hall, Englewood Cliffs, NJ.

Leavitt H J (1986), *Corporate Pathfinders. Building Vision and Values into Organisations*, Dow Jones-Irwin, Homewood, Ill.

Majaro Simon (1988), *International Marketing – A Strategic Approach to World Markets*, Unwin Hyman, London.

— (1991), *The Creative Marketeer*, Butterworth-Heinemann, Oxford.

— (1992), *Managing Ideas for Profit – The Creative Gap*, McGraw Hill, London.

Moss Kanter (1983), *The Changemasters*, Simon & Schuster, New York.

Oliff M C and Marchand D A (1991), 'Strategic Information Management in Global Manufacturing', *European Management Journal*, Vol 9, No 4, Dec.

Parker Marjorie (1990), *Creating Shared Vision*, Dialogue International Ltd, Clarendon Hills, Illinois.

Porter M E (1985), *Competitive Advantage – Creating and Sustaining Superior Performance*, The Free Press, New York.

Quinn J B (1980), *Strategies for Change: Logical Incrementation*, Irwin, Homewood, Ill.

Taylor Robert S (1986), *Value Added Processes in Information Systems*, Ablex, Norwood, NJ.

Von Hippel E (1988), *The Sources of Innovation*, Oxford University Press.

Zuboff Shoshana (1988), *In the Age of the Smart Machine*, Basic Books, New York.

Index